IMPACT@WORK
Volume 2
Achieve Notable Goals

Speaking of impact:

There is only one way to avoid criticism:

Do nothing

Say nothing

And be nothing

Aristotle

From disucssion with readers:

Your focus sends you down a chute – a hundred times a day. Where are you headed?

Options are resilient where you're not in control; commitment, where you are

Bobby Mehdwan

Bobby's had a 25-year career in blue-chip corporate management, coaching individuals and implementing change projects in perhaps a hundred companies in several industries all over the world.

He's seen the best of the best do what they are excellent at on countless production floors, office floors, in office networks and in boardrooms. In the process, he's won and lost many corporate battles and learnt many strategies on exactly what creates impact in the workplace.

Around the middle of his career, Bobby decided to make *impact* a big part of his personal development, wanting to know if there was a way to codify and replicate what the best of the best do naturally in order to elevate impact. Over the years, he found snippets and bit-parts of disconnected learning, but couldn't find a single place where it all came together. So, he made it his challenge to piece together one simple, all-encompassing system for everything he needed to know.

Through observation, systematic learning and practice, and by teaching others he's pulled together impact strategies you can use to significant effect.

Bobby's also a Master of Science and Bachelor of Engineering.

Cover by one designs

Published by 60 Strategies Ltd

Copyright 2016 Bobby Mehdwan. All Rights Reserved. You may not copy, store, distribute or transmit any part of this book by any means—except for brief quotations in reviews—without prior written permission from the publisher.

You may also be interested in the Impact@Work podcast via iTunes or RSS

Find out more about other titles, coaching, training or speaking at 60strategies.com.

Connect

@bobbymehdwan   uk.linkedin.com/in/bobbymehdwan   facebook.com/60strategies

Contents

Introduction and About the Series 1
So, What is Impact? 4
Four Components of Impact 4
How to Start 8
Themes 12
Doing: Achieve Notable Goals 14
   A.   The Art of Triage 23
   Strategy #18: Set Good Goals and Re-Plan Frequently 32
   Strategy #19: Triage Everything to Keep the Important Top of Mind 37
   Strategy #20: Pick Just 1-3 Ways to Spend *All* Your Time 43
   Strategy #21: Look for the 80:20 Pareto Principle in *Everything* 47
   Strategy #22: Know Your Key Success Factors 52
   Strategy #23: Trust the Process 55
   Strategy #24: Make Winning Decisions and Choices 56
   B.   Habit and Routine 71
   Strategy #25: Avoid Willpower. Consistency is King 73
   Strategy #26: You Have No choice 77
   Strategy #27: Be Grateful on Cue Each Day 79
   C.   Batching 85
   Strategy #28: Don't Manage Email 87

    D.   Airplane Mode 95

Strategy #29: Find Focus with Pomodoro, and Avoid Distraction with Internet Blockers 99

Strategy #30: Remain Present to Focus On What's in Front of You 102

Strategy #31: Beware the Multi-Tasking Myth 104

Strategy #32: Rise Early 106

Strategy #33: Manage Your Energy 108

Strategy #34: Speed Date and Try Not to Finish 116

Strategy #35: Persist and Build Competence 119

Strategy #36: Schedule Rest and Play before Work 130

    E.   Diversity and Distraction 139

Strategy #37: Get Creative and Challenge the Status Quo 141

Strategy #38: Cultivate Options and Commitment for Resilience 159

Strategy #39: Learn How to Learn 163

Closing Remarks 169

Introduction and About the Series

First of all, you've probably already covered this introduction if you've read another volume in this series. If that's the case, just take a look at the *Four Components of Impact* below to review the content of this book, then feel free to skip straight to the first strategy further on. These are numbered to precede or continue either side of the other volumes, with 5 dozen straddling the series.

Let's start with an idea – is there anyone out there who doesn't want to make a big impact? Anyone at all?

I think it's fair to assume we all want impact. In fact, we intuitively understand that it's something we all need in order to get ahead.

You probably know and want to emulate people with impact. You may describe them as having a natural flair, which seems to confer them an unfair advantage – unfair in the sense that we've introduced something that's about more than how hard they work, or how good they are at what they do. People with impact overcome obstacles with ease and engage others with grace, exerting influence on everything around them.

But their advantage seems as intangible as charisma.

Now, let's switch to – perhaps – your side of the table.

However hard you work, it can seem like others around you make a bigger impact *and* make it look easy. You have difficult interactions at work where you just can't get through to the people who are important to you – you see things one way and they see it another. You may have felt disadvantaged at some point in your career, as if you just didn't cut it and the feeling may have lingered like a chip on the shoulder – even if, on paper, you had the best accolades for your job. Others, with flair got promoted quicker, leaving you – working hard! You didn't enjoy or get the most out of what you were doing.

It's easy to label this as a confidence problem or consign it to feelings of inferiority in highly competitive workplaces. But if that is the case, what should you do?

Understand that there is limited value in simply trading self-work for recognition in the workplace. Churning out hard work is a hygiene factor (an expected minimum) in the most demanding of workplaces.

Learning to navigate the politics of an organization and understand how people work are more rewarding than *hard* work for more *hard* work.

Supremely impactful people practice impact strategies and thrive.

Impact means you're not just doing your own thing (which is easy) but doing it *with others,* which is much, much harder.

You can only stand out when you master working with others. But first, you have to master being worked with – making it productive and worthwhile for others to work with you. That comes from knowing yourself so you can put your best foot forward.

Mastering interactions may also be the key to enjoying your work. When you reflect, you may discover that you enjoyed, most, the work you did with people who clicked. The opposite is probably just as true.

Knowing yourself isn't the same thing as specialized technical knowledge about your chosen field. That's clearly essential to function effectively and fulfill your role – just as medics must know medicine and managers must know their business. Marketers won't get far without commerciality and so on. But what makes one marketer more impactful than another? Why do some managers make it up the pole faster, all other things being equal? It's not just their technical knowledge, but how they deploy themselves – in a deeply personal sense.

The big challenge for most of us is underinvesting in impact skills while favoring technical skills which look good on a resume. Those however are easily replicated and often abundant. They may confer diminished competitive advantage alone. Furthermore, in many industries, technical knowledge is merely a resource or perhaps a political currency if you know how to acquire and deploy it well, where others are involved.

Nevertheless, from this point on, we'll assume that you have the requisite technical skill, capability or knowledge for your role, because without that, little in this series will elevate you further.

So, What is Impact?

When most people think about impact, they visualize another person dressed to kill, communicating smoothly and powerfully, exuding magnetism and invisibly influencing others around them. Everyone's mesmerized, they turn to jellies and eventually melt into puddles!

Okay, so while the last part's a bit far-fetched, ultimately yes, this sounds like impact. However, this is projection (or delivery) impact and that's just one element of the whole package. Here's the thing – impact sits on top of a solid foundation. Without a foundation it's just fluff and blows around in the wind like in a cardboard TV character.

However, impact is also hard to describe. So, how can we tie it down?

Four Components of Impact

What is it that impactful people do? Are they born naturals?

That's certainly what I've always believed. And perhaps the answer is yes, by virtue of personality. But, it's almost certain that everything they know was learnt at some point, whether or not they were consciously aware of it – or even care to admit it.

If you practice impact, however, you'll be in rarified company that's difficult for rivals to replicate.

Technical skills and knowledge aside, some traits shared by impactful people are:

1. High levels of self-awareness and an ability to negotiate through challenging circumstances
2. An ability to focus on areas of strength utilizing tailored systems and processes to achieve goals
3. Confidence to project powerfully and influence others for the best outcomes
4. Highly strategic, competing vigorously when required and able to ward off rivals effortlessly.

In Volume 1: *Connecting: Self-awareness Behavior & Motivation* we saw how getting others to act for you is the very foundation of impact. We learnt what moves people – including you – and how your behavior elicits or hinders action. We understood how to stay the course so that you and others could make a positive impact in difficult situations. Self-awareness gave you some of the essentials of presence.

Now, let's take a more detailed look at this book: Volume 2: *Doing: Achieve Notable Goals.* In this book, you'll learn to do what you do best and how to do it the best you can.

Impactful people are effective at what they do and focused on doing what they are effective at. They:

- Choose to focus on strengths instead of allowing the choice of others to dominate
- Do what they do really well using tailored systems, processes, habits and routines to boost productivity and achieve the outcomes they want, while anticipating downsides and risks
- Limit or avoid frivolous distractions
- Create without relying on blind faith, hope, motivation or vision, but heed convention where necessary
- Know how to push through the obstacles in their path.

We'll look at turning your motivations from Volume 1 into notable goals in Volume 2, so you can create unbeatable substance with solid foundations.

When you move on to Volume 3 you'll learn the secrets of *Projecting: Communicate & Lead with Power & Presence.* You will learn to lead and face the world in a compelling way by telling good stories about what drove you to achieve your goals in Volumes 1 & 2, utilizing great structure to get others on-side. We'll dissect leadership, communication and negotiation.

Finally, in Volume 4: *Competing: Secure your Limelight* we'll look at how to stack systems in your favor and prevent others encroaching and stealing your limelight, created in the first three Volumes in the series. You'll learn how to leapfrog and carefully manage out rivals looking for a share of your spoils.

That's impact!

Four Components of Impact

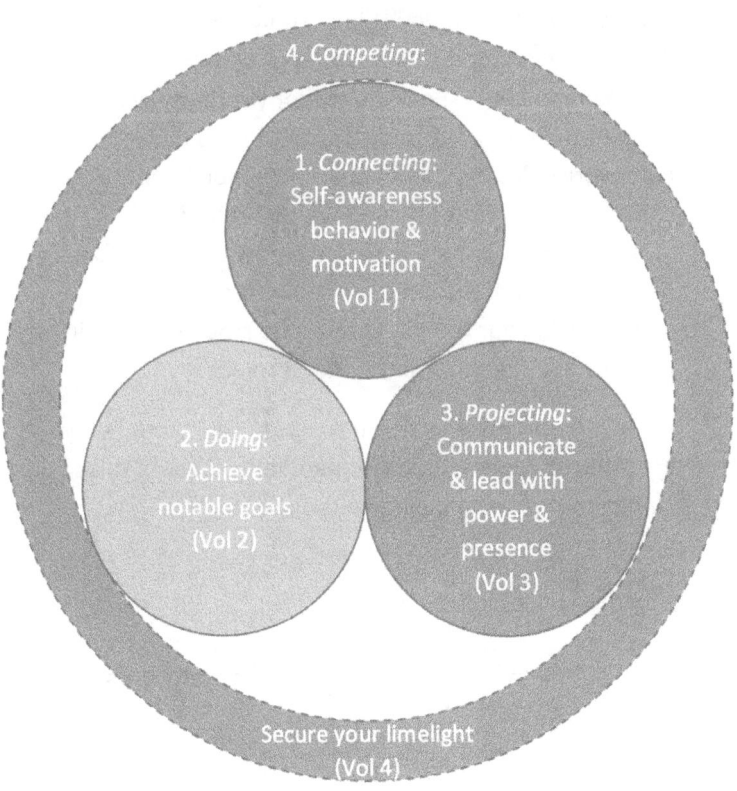

But wait a moment! You're up against a lot here!

Impact is clearly a skill set in its own right, just like knowing how to play an instrument, or code a program or develop products. When practiced over a lifetime, it will push and keep you streets ahead of the pack.

Without any of these strategies under your belt, you're going to work every day without speaking the language of elites. If you think simply turning up, or doing what you do best, or training to improve skills, or putting in the hours, or doing what your boss wants, is enough to make a big impact, you're probably in for a big surprise. No matter what your capability or competence at your job, you *will be* limited and manipulated by others who know how to make a bigger personal impact. With most or all of the following strategies in your toolkit, you will be a powerhouse in virtually any organization or marketplace.

If you think that you're not in this game, yet you are going to work with other people, you *are* in this game. You're being played without accepting it.

How to Start

Several people I have coached over the years have said: *If only I knew this when I started...*

I couldn't agree more. In a sense, the series is written for my – relatively naïve – twenty something self, starting the world of work, clutching degree certificates and feeling like they meant everything.

Have you ever thought: *Wouldn't it be awesome if I could start again with all that I now know?* Well, start today.

I'll bet that one or two strategies make a big impression on you right off the bat. Go with them – you are adaptable to circumstance and not a slave to preference. Like coaching, read one per day or week – say on your daily commute – then set your priorities on your daily agenda (I wrote the conversation styles in my notebook and left that page open during meetings). Ask a coach (or anyone) to observe you in action and provide feedback. That'll make the tips and tricks easy to digest and practical to implement. Repeat until they become habitual.

Stick with a strategy anywhere from a month to six, until it becomes automatic and feels normal.

In this series, I'll use myriad examples from the consumer tech, the arts (particularly story-telling) and other industries to illustrate the strategies outlined in each volume. Nevertheless, some will make immediate sense while others will come into play when you move on up.

Self-awareness alone will begin an internal change process that will show on the outside almost immediately – within days.

The series tries to move you quickly into *doing*, because that's vastly more important than simply reading, cogitating, or feeling motivated. I'll give you the *so what?* straight and easy, with real life lessons from some of the toughest work situations.

You'll find a key, which may help you prioritize the strategies:

Easy!	Easy to understand with immediate impact!
Persist	Persist and remain alert. It will deliver!

If this is the first time you've seen this material, it might hurt your head in places as you grapple. Persist and learn more about something that may not resonate at first.

Even if you find something familiar, just re-read it, because reminders are helpful when heads are frantic and memories fade. Consistency and persistence are key.

Now, have a journal handy – it's really important to try the questions if you really want to get the most out of this.

Take your time: remember that *presence* is a panacea. Presence builds resilience when combined with an understanding of your *emotional center* and – as you will read later in Volume 2 – mutually exclusive *options*.

Phew! Now try the exercise below. Look at the following diagram and try to figure out which inner box is a darker shade of grey.

Our Reality is our Perception[1] And Context is King – Which Inner Box is a Lighter Shade of Grey – Left or Right? (answer in the footnote)[2]

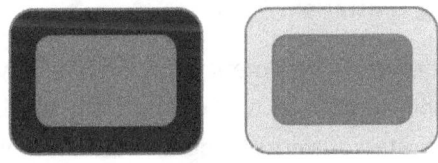

Did you get the puzzle?

No two people experience the world in the same way and our priorities, life position and context are all different.

To someone who has everything, everything else looks like opportunity. Conversely, to someone who's simply trying to survive, the exact same things can look like loss prevention. Your context is vital and a strategy may or may not make sense, depending on your life position.

---

[1] New research suggests that perception actually hides reality from us - but that's a whole different science! For now, accept that *our* reality is *our* perception (though perhaps not the *real thing*).

[2] Both inner boxes are the same shade of grey, though the context (outside shades) are different. Nevertheless, you see them differently. Our brains understand anything only by virtue of anything's relationship to anything else and not in absolute terms. Reality looks different to each of us.

Themes

You'll probably notice an underlying theme or two which may surprise you.

Firstly, being impactful requires you to challenge yourself and others – constantly seeking out the best way to do things, rather than just accepting the way things are. This can result in a lot of saying *no* **and feeling contrarian.**

Consider a statement from the late Steve Jobs, founder and vaunted ex-CEO of Apple and perhaps the most celebrated business leader in modern times: 'What I chose *not* to do was just as important to me as what I *did* do.' Now there's someone with impact!

Paradoxically, his sentiment is of increasing importance for all of us compared to even just half a century back. We now live in a distraction economy which presents us with excessive choice (partly the fault of Steve Jobs, in my view). A lot arrived with the internet, and it's now in our pockets on our smartphones. Every time we're in the company of others and turn to notifications from distant corners of the world, we relinquish easy opportunities to make an impact on those around us. However big or small, these moments add up. Notifications immediately throw us out of presence and when we act like this continuously, we go through a lot of our lives on our own islands with pretend connections. The benefit of saying no will often be freedom to be impactful in our own unique ways where it really counts.

Secondly, you may at first find the strategies make you feel self-centered, or even manipulative in some cases. That's a perfectly normal, but it's not the aim at all. You'll be finding your own voice.

You will also undoubtedly come across some unpalatable truths, particularly when we talk about getting the right things done in Volumes 3 and 4; but also throughout, as we unpack bias and influence. Fear not!

Questions

Before diving in, think now about what impact means to you and what you most want to work on. This will help you to home in on your priorities.

1. What does impact mean to me? ....
2. What do I want to work most on? ....
3. Who could support or help me? ....

Doing: Achieve Notable Goals

If you've read Volume 1, you've understood your motivations and know how fear and negativity bias limits you. You now have a huge leg up in achieving the big notable goals which strike fear into the hearts of others.

So, where does this book come from? Simple – it's based on an idea by my buddy Mark. He's a smart guy and an accomplished manager with a strong work ethic and here's what he said, bleary eyed at the end of another busy week:

> "Like everyone else, I work hard, week after week – but sometimes it's hard to know what I've achieved at the end of the month, or even this year."

I can tell you, he's not alone. At the time, I would have asked him to think about whether he was doing the *right things*, or just doing the *wrong things right*. I think he would have said, 'Just doing my job.' He was burning the midnight oil and peddling as fast as he could.

Impactful people are quite deliberate in what they do and use systems and processes to help them achieve the right things. They don't, for the most part, just luck out or see rewards for simply working hard.

Often their story is one of preparation underneath the radar – for years – so they're prepared to strike when the perfect opportunity arises.

Though most of us will never get lucky, the ones who do simply see opportunity when it arises and are willing to take a leap when their time comes.

In Volume 2, I've distilled key strategies that the world's highest achievers have used since the beginning of time to achieve the highest impact through productivity. Volume 2 is all about getting you to do the right stuff, so you're ready when it will count most. Getting the right stuff done will give you a solid foundation for huge impact.

A fundamental theme is clearing your desk for what's important for you – that is, *avoiding* distraction rather than wasting a monumental amount of energy fighting it with misguided willpower.

If you've read Volume 1, you'll have understood your motivations – you'll have visions of what you love to do, or at least don't hate.

When those ideas are clear, compelling and persistent, you cannot help but be drawn in, provided there are no obstacles or diversions. Compelling ideas are like opened doors, discovered paths, gentle descents, slippery slopes or chutes to somewhere – it may well be impossible to avoid something that grabs you in this way (warning – you must be exceptionally careful what ideas you are repeatedly and frequently exposed to!)

This is the reason I've suggested, in the introduction, that you journal your thoughts as you go.

Writing helps to clarify your ideas and requires attention, which then cements them in your head.

Assuming you've now discovered your motivation, be prepared to spend 99% of your time doing the doing, so you'd better love it for what it is!

And while motivation is driven by feeling good (or bad), realize that it's just a movement of dopamine (a feel-good neuro-chemical), or cortisol (a feel-bad neuro-chemical) in the brain. Highs and lows are simply induced chemical reactions inside your head – induced by yourself, politicians, leaders, advertisers or other story-tellers. They are simply pre-packaged primers, sold by visionaries like caffeine is by big coffee and nicotine by big tobacco. What's more, neuro-chemicals require no licensing, production, storage or distribution on the producer's part! They are there to manipulate what you do every moment of every day.

Dopamine and cortisol may be the only things that get us out of bed and get our wallets out of pockets. But after administration, bold vision and motivation *act* too much like a fair wind at best. They simply don't stack up to anything useful on their own – mainly because they're incredibly difficult to hold accountable, unlike specific outcomes.

The second problem, in the corporate world at least, is that vision is normally vague, non-specific and often incomprehensible and guaranteed to be distant from day to day reality.

To make vision and motivation relevant, then, they must be simple, compelling and frequently top of mind.

But still, that's not enough! When the cold light of day burns away a vision induced high, you may be left with commitments and expectations you're not actually equipped to deliver. This is the commonest story of failed ambition. It's all your unmet New Year resolutions on a plate. Many great expectations stop here. No further reading necessary.

This book, however, is designed to keep you moving effortlessly towards notable goals where hordes of people fall by the wayside.

So remember: **Vision is a spark, but it's action which greases that slippery slope.**

Like the steering on a car, vision may keep you moving in a particular direction, but you need a good engine and a foot on a pedal to generate anything even half useful. You need pistons working consistently and hard to fight friction and inertia – and pistons that pull you free from the gravity of other agendas which yank your attention in different directions.

Once you orient yourself north, south, east or west, you'd be best served by parking vision and focusing your energy on the well-oiled engine and your foot on that pedal, moving one step at a time towards your goal.

When you act on an idea consistently, you lower yourself into productive habits. Acting this way becomes self-reinforcing and with persistence, your vision will begin to dominate your worldview. We learnt in Volume 1, that taking full responsibility for how we spend our time is necessary for big impact.

Rely on habit, skill and action then, because together, these always trump – by a long shot – the perceived wisdom of vision and motivation in actually *creating* anything.

How you go about doing that is the subject of this book.

A Productivity System for Impact[3]

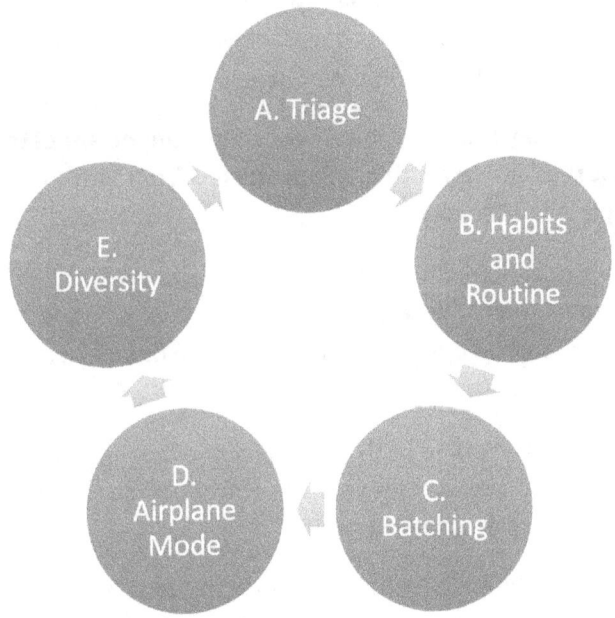

You can implement this cycle daily, weekly, monthly or even annually! The best way is to tailor it for your specific needs at the time.

---

[3] A. Narrowing. Neutralize distraction, Prioritize and focus on 2-3 things, 80:20 rule, Organize notes and ideas, Deflect and delegate, Negotiate priorities, Set expectations. B. Cementing. Daily autopilot, Eliminate choice, Fundamentals, Essentials, Non negotiables (even with self), Avoid decisions. C. Maximizing. Relentless efficiency. D. Closed and Focused. Energy withdrawn, Avoid distraction, Far from the madding crowd! E. Open & Curious. Seek distraction and diversity, Open to opportunism, Listen, Read and learn, Organize and combine, Create options, Seek feedback, Jot notes and ideas, In with the madding crowd!

On a busy project, for instance, I would often be closed for the first half the day and open for the second half – attending to messages while also triaging the following day. I might take the following week to meet clients, attend conferences or develop a product.

Key principle: whatever's most important gets absorbed into a routine and protected from the vagaries of the day.

At home, for instance, I may write every morning then take care of admin or marketing in the afternoons. I'd open snail mail and settle bills once a month.

At the time of this writing, I'm batching a range of content creation this year then moving on to batch publishing the following year.

When we get busy, it's easy to spend all our time in Mode E (open to the world). We don't find the time or a consistently effective path back to the other states – which is where it all happens! Running around simply fills our time because continuous changes in our environment grab our attention. We're wired to pay attention to noise (even if that's all it is) but by the time we realize, it's already too late – attention and energy are already spent.

Equally, it's just as easy to get stuck in Mode D (Closed). The transition from D to E – and vice versa – where necessary, can be quite a switch. It's like pulling a different set of muscles which haven't been in operation for a period of time. It can be helpful to create some empty space in between to help the transition – perhaps put your things away to signal the mental shift required.

If you read about Operating Modes in Volume 1, you might recognize that Mode E somewhat resembles the Promoter (or Finder) style, in the sense that it's open to the world and expression of ideas. This might be the mode of Carers too. It should also be obvious that these modes aren't where the work's done, so you're unlikely to be productive if this is how you spend the majority of your time! Modes A and B can be likened to Controller (or Minder), whereas Modes C and D most closely resembles the Analyst (or Grinder). As you learnt in Volume 1, it's helpful to move between modes to make the most of your moments.

Questions

Before diving in, think now about what productivity means to you, and what you most want to work on. This will help you to home in on your priorities.

1. Which of the above productivity elements do I most need to work on? ....

2. Impact of ignoring it: ....

3. What would I tackle second or third? ....

A. The Art of Triage

The aim of triage is to narrow your focus on activities which are supremely important. When asked at a dinner once: *what was the most important single factor in their success?* both Bill Gates and Warren Buffet replied with one word: "focus."[4] The simple fact is, that you get more of whatever it is you focus on. If you observe your thought patterns and behavior, you'll observe that you walk straight into whatever's top of mind, as if it were everything. This is a trait built right into the human brain.

At a global level, think of the important activities as the items which must find their way onto your résumé (which has extremely limited space). These items have to be worthy of discussion at a future imaginary job interview, otherwise their value must be questioned.

You're looking for signal amongst all the noise when you triage.

Picture this: You've done the thinking, you know what you want to do, so you start off with good intent; but a week later you're onto something completely different.

---

[4] You can read about this in Warren Buffet's biography, The Snowball by Alice Shroeder

You may not have even touched whatever you said you wanted to focus on. This is common, but no one's impactful operating this way.

The best way I know to alleviate this problem is to write down what you want AND review what you wrote each day. Why? Because looking at your priorities on paper keeps you objective and reminds you that you're on the path that *you* chose whenever you feel uncertain about where you're heading. You may argue that your role is to keep multiple plates spinning – and so be it if that's the case, but just remember that no-one ever got famous for firefighting.

As life moves into your day, you will take frequent gusts of wind against your sails and you'll be blown off course easily. Impactful people learn to stay the course through difficulties and all the diversions that work and life present.

When you're not using a system to help you, you're almost guaranteed to spend too much time on menial, unimportant things which may only suit someone else's agenda. Why? Recency is at work inside your head to keep certain things top of mind. You may also feel compelled to act consistently with whatever commitments you made earlier – whether or not they still represent a worthy priority later.

Avoid these traps by first *creating* some distance and perspective from whatever comes at you. Second, have a few options in your choices – this avoids attachment to any single course of action (you're avoiding what's known as the consistency principle). Those are exactly what a triage permits.

In this strategy, you'll learn to triage *everything* that comes in. Simply clearing your desk of crud makes way for the good stuff where you'll maximize your impact. You'll avoid wasting time and energy on things you dislike or you aren't cut out for. Over time, you'll have laser focus on what's important and avoid your time being devoured by necessary evils like marketing comms, software updates, travel bookings, walking through airports, sifting emails and everything else that comes with corporate process.

This applies to your personal life too – buying on Amazon, listing on eBay, paying bills, etc. Think about it – you wouldn't want this ragbag of items accounting for your time, would you? Would you like one or all of these as the only accolade on your tombstone someday? *He was really quite good at replying to email, or, he had five stars on eBay – that's all I can recall!!* How does that sound? Don't let this sort of stuff devour hours, days, weeks or years of an otherwise notable career.

If you look carefully at these things, you'll realize quickly that they're mostly about *you* propping up *other* little industries. You're serving someone else's agenda operating like this and these items don't necessarily contribute to your impact at work or on the world in order to make it a better place.

But that doesn't mean you can avoid some of them altogether (though you may at least try). You'd clearly be derailed for avoiding email communication altogether and may even miss important opportunities. First, then, you have to deflect what you can, second you delegate what must still get done but not your priority and third you must box in what's left on *your* plate, so it doesn't grow and devour your energy.

This requires *continuous* awareness and the willingness to deflect distractions. If you learn to do this one thing consistently I'd guess you'll emulate the top 5% of impactful people.

Why Triage?

Consider just how much more we have coming at us than *ever* before. It's more than our heads have evolved to handle. The UK's Daily Telegraph reported on a 2007 study by the University of Southern California, which found that we received around 40-newspapers worth of information daily in 1986, but this had ballooned to 174 by 2007. Just a hundred years ago, a lifetime worth of reading was 50 books at the most.

Technology seems to have transformed office life from placid and methodical in the 20th century, to frantic and mercurial in the 21st, leaving many of us feeling like we spend our days chasing balls, kicked from pillar to post by whatever's top of the corporate mind. Technology's also opened the door to always-on busy work which provides the illusion of productivity, when in reality, there's often a lot of frantic paddling under the surface simply to tread water. We use our phones habitually – on average five hours per day – checking notifications up to eighty-five times daily.

We now have **multiple channels** of information and communication, incessantly bombarding us with noise – continuous micro-news and advertising content which is repeated on websites, television, radio, social networks, in emails and so on. All these are now in our pockets too and demand attention all day every day.

The internet and smartphones have also allowed billions of **new producers** of demands for our attention to generate their own flavor of trivia on websites, social networks and video sharing sites. Just ten or twenty years ago, gatekeepers may have released relevant and useful content on agenda. Good or bad, it was rarely overwhelming.

Then there's **high refresh**. All of the above content can now be re-packaged as *new*, quickly and cheaply. A high refresh rate feigns manufactured urgency, but our brains can't help thinking that it's all important.

But there's both good and bad news (pun intended) above. The good is that you can normally spot agendas behind high refresh. Advertising and promotion are key to commercial and news sites, where keeping eyeballs glued to paid for ads is often more important than the content of many sites themselves. In addition, the economic value of companies, especially those in tech based services, is increasingly grounded in their ability to sell habit forming products and services.

In corporate life, someone nagging is almost always someone wanting to tick-off a to-do-list item or to self-promote (get good at asking when something *really* requires attention and completion, so you can weed out and negotiate away feigned urgency).

Perhaps worst of all, once we're hooked to this way of being, we're unable to cope with its absence – try putting your technology away for a day, or even just an hour while sitting alone! Mobile devices, for all their liberation, have made many of us unproductively distractible and anxious, fearful of missing out. It's as if we no longer tolerate even the smallest amount of quiet time alone with ourselves. If you look around the office, I'll bet you can see who's in this camp. For instance, I recently ran a project with two very smart, high-demand colleagues who couldn't stop looking at their phone and laptop respectively. The result was that one never produced anything (groaning about being spread too thin) and the other always handed in deliverables late. If companies want to get the best out of employees, they might help themselves by understanding individual working styles and the impact of technology on productivity.

So, multiple channels of information, new habit forming producers, a high-refresh rate and personal agendas result in a lot of noise. What's worse is that this sets up a cubed rate of information growth. The result is an inevitable dilution of our personal impact in our priorities. If you don't triage at some level, you're simply wandering around on a lost battlefield every day.

The Technology Revolution: Drowning in Trivia, and Why We Need Systems to Separate the Signal from a Bonanza of Noise

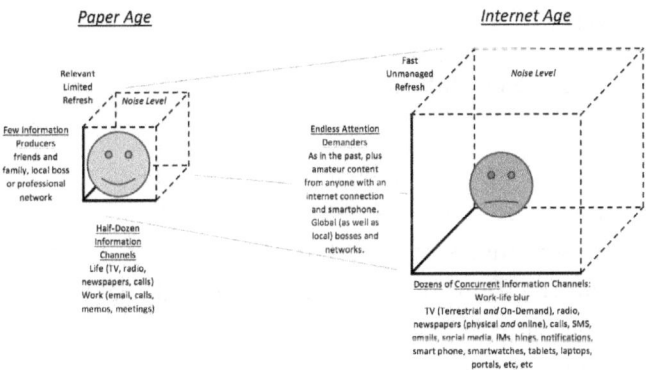

You can see from the diagram that not only do we have many more producers of information, there are many more channels through which it arrives.

Much of it is also superfluous to our interests or needs in the moment or simply regurgitates what we already know while looking for an audience.

We also find that *everything* is instantly refreshed simply by pulling down on the screen in front of us, or coming back to work after a long weekend.

So, how can we deal with this? The first thing to recognize is that a lot of the *extra* information produced by the internet age may be redundant. A large proportion of content is specifically designed to be evergreen and habit forming and therefore keeps reappearing in different guises, time after time.

Secondly, of course, you should get into the practice of triage, before the moment of consumption or action.

First, some truths:

- Urgent things pretend importance. Think of newsfeeds and limited-time promotions
- Urgent things demand your attention even if not worthy. Think of phones dinging with the latest social media update
- Truly important things rarely, if ever, seek attention. Think about your ambition once to write that book or learn an instrument. How often did that idea ding or ping?
- If you're not making choices about your priorities, the world makes them for you and pulls you in its direction
- You can't be objective and efficient about how to spend your time if you manage your commitments in your head. In fact, the brain is tuned to focus on things which are unresolved, unfinished or recent. This proves vital to advertisers, marketers and demanders for attention.

What's top of mind *feels* more significant than something old; and what's top of mind is usually whatever just cropped up.

Because our brains can't hold much water, they tend to focus on recent occurrences. Unfortunately, the brain's best strategy is to behave like a 1990s internet pop-up browser.

We'll see how you can actually use this to your advantage later, but for now understand that your head just wants to chase whatever's shouting loudest or came up last.

At the same time, demanders of attention will also knowingly pull on a reciprocity bias.

We usually feel inclined to help or respond to someone even if their need is perfectly deferrable, because deferral feels like issuing a rebuttal – so we don't say *no* when we sometimes should.

What if we have hundreds of new things coming at us each day from the moment we open the curtains and let the world into our heads? It's easy to see how important things remain on the bench or forgotten completely. Once you stop something, overcoming the inertia to get going again can feel like double the effort.

Strategy #18[5]: Set Good Goals and Re-Plan Frequently

If you've read Volume 1, you'll have understood the importance of motivation and how working *with it* is essential for big impact. Working against it puts an invisible ceiling in your way.

In order to set the *right* goals, first understand what fundamentally motivates you. Set repeated goals which give you a dopamine hit (a feel-good neuro-chemical) and not cortisol. The latter drives you when you're constantly fighting fires and tackling problems.

Without clear goals, you'll be sucked in by whatever tractor beam comes along to grab your attention (or lure your wallet) in any particular moment. You've read about the staggering array of diversions available to us in the smartphone age. Without goals, you may not even realize when you're off your path and simply clearing weeds on someone else's.

In contrast, when goals are clear and compelling, like a grand vision, you cannot help but be drawn down the path you open up.

---

[5] Numbering continued from strategies 1-17 in Volume 1

Your goals are your direction of impact. Will it be head-on, or a near miss?

Here are a few things to bear in mind, as you set goals:

- **Set daily and weekly goals for how you want to *spend your time*.** While long-term goals are your compass, it's daily and weekly goals which provide the momentum and add up.

    Daily and weekly goals set your focus and keep your attention on all the manageable *now* moments, which will stack up day by day to become your long-term goals. Daily goals are the footsteps which take you up the mountain.

    By making how you want to spend your time, your goal each day, your head stays in what you control. Instead, if you're focusing on goals as achievements you may find yourself trying to will to life that which you don't control – at least not fully. That's madness. Enjoying what you *do,* as you do it, keeps you present.

- **Diarize your daily and weekly goals**. It's easy to get sucked into one of your priorities and allow others to languish. And the longer they languish, the harder it is to re-light them.

    Your aim, then, is to put daily and weekly goals in the diary to ensure the wheels keep spinning. You want to avoid having to repeatedly overcome the inertia of re-starting something. Keep the wheels spinning and you'll achieve your goals faster and easier.

- **Focus entirely on the *first* next step**. That's the one thing you can do today – now. Remember in the introduction we said that presence is an ally? This is how you get presence to count for you big time.

    Your goal will simply arise – or not – from a stack of all the *now* moments. In fact, it *never* happens any other way.

- **Plan backwards from the goal in three to four steps**. Ask yourself, what's the one big thing that must happen before the goal is reached? Then continue working backwards to today.

    Planning backwards avoids a lot of busy work and contingents – things that must happen first before you can proceed – which you tend to get when planning left to right. What you'll find is the critical path – the 20% which really moves the needle – amongst the 80% busyness you can conjure up when planning left to right.

    Example: I can't get to step 3 of my plan until I do these *10 things*. Those are contingents. So, you set about doing 10 things, feeling productive and looking busy. You might even wear busyness like a badge of honor. But when you apply the 80:20 rule below you may come to realize that a lot of what you get with left to right planning alone is unnecessary.

So, whenever you get the urge to plan left to right, make sure you re-plan right to left – looking for and cutting the fat in your plans.

- **Anticipate challenges and obstacles, then allow back some contingency.** Plans fail at first contact for a great number of reasons, but not least because we either don't see – or avoid seeing – what's just off-stage waiting to scupper our plans. It's the result of an inbuilt planning fallacy which we talked about in Volume 1.

    We also fail to understand where we are in the competency cycle – we may not have the requisite skills and capabilities we need. Do we realize how long it takes to develop them? No – we proceed with gusto and hubris. We'll talk more about this later.

Rip up your plans frequently and keep asking: 'Is there a quicker, easier, better, way to do this?' Then be honest about what you need.

Questions

Think about what you just learnt and write down your answers. You're more likely to action something important if you write it down.

1. What fundamentally motivates me? ....
2. My goals do or don't align with my motivators? ....
3. Am I more outcome focused (achievement) than activity focused (daily): ....
4. How does that impact my attention and progress towards my goals? ....

Strategy #19: Triage Everything to Keep the Important Top of Mind

What we're going to do is:

1. **Write our commitments but organize and manage them in a triage center and;**
2. **Be extremely deliberate about *Not* To Dos as well as *Yes* To Dos.**

   One of the best tools for this job is an Important/Urgent matrix, using a principle coined by former US President Eisenhower. It's simply a tabular format To Do list, but this one's a big deal – trust me.

If you want your days to be fulfilled and productive, this is a system to make it so.

   If you read Volume 1, you'll remember that we talked about changing your experience as the way to change your limiting beliefs. The Eisenhower matrix will send you straight into the kinds of experience you want and those which are good for you.

   You may, for the first time ever, really feel like the days are adding up to what you wanted when you start to use this strategy.

Important Urgent Triage System (Eisenhower Matrix) – Put Your To Dos on Here

High Benefit (B) of doing or **Big** Loss (L) from avoiding these things

Important but NOT Urgent	Important AND Urgent (do now)
Schedule these and turn into habits	*1-3 items to focus on each day*
• Work: Networking, visibility, training, mentoring and coaching, business development • Life: Whatever you'd like to see on your tombstone, fitness, long term health, family, friends, life goals	• Work: Your immediate work, tomorrow's presentation, looming deadline • Life: Maintenance essentials: car, house, piano practice, immediate health
NOT Important NOR Urgent	**Urgent but NOT Important**
Avoid anything that wouldn't stand <u>alone</u> on your tombstone	*Avoid, simplify, delegate or outsource anything that's manufactured urgency, or a doubtful use of your time – but still needs doing.*
• Work: Anything that doesn't add to the story of your résumé i.e. you can't sell it on • Life: social media, marketing and advertising, material purchases (unless they earn you a living).	• Work: Anything that doesn't support your résumé, but is still necessary e.g. corporate process, meetings and corporate comms, expense claims, timesheets, most email • Life: social media, promotions, paying bills

Low benefit (b) of doing, or **small** loss (l) from avoiding these things

Write down and triage *everything* that comes at you or from within you.

Do only things that you've written in their rightful place. This is crucial when you're learning this technique and is still crucial until the important takes primacy and becomes habit.

Include emailing, calls, social media, reminders, and so on, remembering that you can also be your own worst enemy in this respect – dreaming up new things to do or think about before delivering what you've already committed. Promoters must be especially aware of this. (Read about Promoters in Operating Modes in Volume 1).

At first, the matrix might feel like a steam-powered way of doing things in the age of always-on and instant everything – but that's partly its purpose. Always-on, instant everything utilizes your momentum to prop up the pointless. Choosing your pace will lead you to find focus and do a few things well under tight pressure rather than a thousand things poorly around the clock.

Review the triage daily or twice daily and move items around as warranted.

Once in a while, purge the triage and make sure that the important items find their way back onto the blank page. Use the 80:20 Pareto principle to help you cut the fat. More on that below.

This singular practice of writing it all down will quickly open your eyes to the sheer volume of useless

commitments you're making to others and yourself, that you also never had any real chance of fulfilling.

The top half:

- Your focus should always be on the top right of the chart, and all your top right items should be *immediate* actions or activities, and not project titles or other catch-alls. You're trying to focus on what you can do *now – today*
- When a new urgent and important item comes in, move something from top right to top left *temporarily*
- When the top right clears, move over something from top left temporarily
- Have the triage at hand when you finish one activity or have spare time. It will keep you on the right track instead of being swayed by whatever noise comes in. After a few weeks, you will probably find the system beginning to work for you
- Paradoxically, when things start to work, boredom and distraction can move in, because you are (like the rest of us) an experience seeking creature. Understand that this is normal. But you also can't build a coherent story chasing random experiences, so whip out the triage and remind yourself that you're on the right path that you chose. If not, change it. If nothing else, just actively make choices.

The bottom half:

- Get the unimportant out of your head and onto the page as quickly as you can
- Remind yourself where the crud sits whenever it rears its ugly head repeatedly
- Treat email as glorified To Dos which everyone else fills out for you. Don't manage email or social media, but note down those which are important enough to process in the right place on the triage. Discard, ignore or, better still, filter out the rest so they remain out of sight. We'll cover email later
- **Get used to taking small losses on some items that fall off the bottom of the chart. This will free you to focus on big gains at the top.**

Finally, batch similar or concurrent activities to be as efficient as possible. For example: running an errand while you're in the vicinity of a location for something else on the list.

When you're not reacting immediately, perspective will pleasantly surprise you by showing you how much you can batch for maximum efficiency – particularly the necessary crud.

Though we'll talk more about batching below, all I will say now is that you have already begun batching with this strategy. Triage will help you make better choices over the totality of your commitments because they are now in one place and prioritized top-down, rather than in multiple places and popping up at different times to scatter your attention.

Questions

Think about what you just learnt and write down your answers. You're more likely to action something important if you write it down.

1. I am/am not sufficiently good at prioritizing: ....
2. Where could I most improve? ....
3. Where will I maintain my Eisenhower matrix (paper/PC/Smartphone notes)? ....
4. How often I will review it? ....

Strategy #20: Pick Just 1-3 Ways to Spend *All* Your Time

If you read Volume 1, you'll be clear on what motivates you – what's important to you.

In this strategy, we're not talking outcomes, but simply how you want to spend your days over the next 6 months, 12 months, or even the rest of your life.

Aim for 3 life and work priorities to give yourself half a chance of devoting enough energy to them. If you pick 5, you'll be spread so thin that you'll probably dilute your impact.

Each day, start your day by thinking about which of the 1-3 top-right items is *the* priority for *today*. What does that mean?

Without being too precise in the numbers, it means that, of all the things you could do, what's the *one thing* that'll really move the needle the most today, or right now? Perhaps to get you over a challenge at work, or to work towards the one thing you'd have on your tombstone at the end of your days.

Just one. Be brutal.

Begin the day with this question from the moment you get up. Avoid anything else – whether from the outside or inside (both are equally derailing). To make this work, avoid morning meetings – they simply open the door for *other's* agendas to dominate your day. It's the surest way I know to have your priorities derailed.

This is the best way to maintain control and avoid overwhelming yourself when things get extremely demanding. It helps you avoid the energy-sapping paradox of choice. You're avoiding the illusion of wanting (or needing) to control everything in your sphere of influence. It's easy to follow busy work, live in 'overwhelm' and wear it all like a badge of honor. But I hope you now see that that's a futile route to impact.

Your time will be diluted beyond repair and there's no recovery button for time badly spent.

What you'll find when your one thing is covered early in the day, is that the second and third thing will happen with ease too – if they are important. Why? There's a psychological boost from winning on your priorities early in the day.

Your aim is to have a portfolio of mutually exclusive activities that you enjoy – that is, they don't depend on each other. We'll look at the reason for the portfolio when we talk about the power of options later.

Do you want to spend your days on X type of project or Y project? Do you want to spend all your time at work or some of it learning something – say a sport or instrument? Do you want to be selling or delivering?

These are simply choices that you have to make, then go after. Anything else should only get a look in once these are done – do them *first* each day.

Let me tell you now that you'll be astonished at how much you begin to enjoy your days, feel more productive and less regretful with this type of focus. This is because, when you enjoy what you do, you will be highly *present*. Conversely, when you are continually outcome focused, you're rarely present. We know you can't have a big impact that way.

And don't confuse your 3-5 things with daily tasks, goals or vision. Use goals and vision to orient yourself at the outset, but that's all. It might sound obvious, but it's how you spend your days that will add up to your goals and vision – or lack thereof.

Let's say you're in sales, in a client-service business. Your goal might be to have 10 new clients by year end. A way to *spend your time* might then be use 3 days per week to contact and meet new leads, and two days managing a sales pipeline.

That effort compounds quickly if you *spend your time* in this way *consistently*.

In fact, it's the only way to achieve your goals. Sounds obvious, doesn't it? Even if you don't achieve the goals, you will have enjoyed your days in sales if that's how you wanted to spend your time. There's no downside.

So how do you stick with this regimen and avoid being blown off course by attention hogs? Start with your Eisenhower matrix which we discussed above.

Questions

Have a go at these questions.

1. From my Eisenhower matrix, the 1-3 things I must do daily/weekly/monthly (these remain on the matrix as a visual reminder): ....
2. The things I will relegate to *not important* in the grand scheme of things. I'm willing to accept a small loss if these get forgotten: ....

Strategy #21: Look for the 80:20 Pareto Principle in *Everything*

You've almost certainly heard of the 80:20 principle – it applies to pretty much everything we come across. You could also call it the law of diminishing returns.

It says that you should bet on a whopping 80% of your efforts delivering diminished or little return.

You must always lookout for the 20% of events which count for 80% of your results *first* and not the other way around.

But there's a paradox (or a bummer) if you're aiming high. You can make huge strides early in any project (covering 80% of the ground during the initial 20% of the assault) but watch with incredulity as the ratio turns on you. You'll have to go deeper, first up to your waist, then up to the neck in treacle in order to cover the last 20% and get your work over the line.

***Expect* the last 20% to take 80% of your effort. That's what giving 100% means.**

Another way to accept this reality is exploring nine dead ends in order to find the one path that works. Giving 100% is like panning for gold. The 80% is writing five drafts of your report, the final 20% is whittling it down to its true essence. Build that into your timetable.

But don't let this paradox blind you. The business world (and most of life) is, however, about economics and viability first.[6] No one goes into business to *perform* first – they can do that as a hobby. Perfection only works if a business can monetize it by the hour. Giving 100% isn't necessarily time well spent.

When you look at products and services, you see that we have scores of everything – whether iPhones, earplugs or fast cars, or even jobs – and if it isn't one of them, it'll *always* be another. So, viability really counts, particularly in arenas where switching costs are low. This gave birth to the idea of a Minimal Viable Product for new ideas. An MVP is never conceived as 100%.

In his book *The Long Tail* Chris Anderson explains how companies like Amazon are increasingly turning non-top-dog products and services into the new top dogs. Digital distribution of everything from résumés to products and services is changing what it means to be top. It seems perfection counts less and less, while viability becomes more and more important. Most things simply aren't viable with 100% effort.

On the other hand, there can't be 10 Usain Bolts or a score of Mozarts (pun intended). You're either top dog, or not, in those kind of endeavors. They are all about performance.

---

[6] If you think perfection is necessary in business, just look at early iterations of smartwatches (or iphones) to debunk that myth.

A Normal Distribution (not to scale)

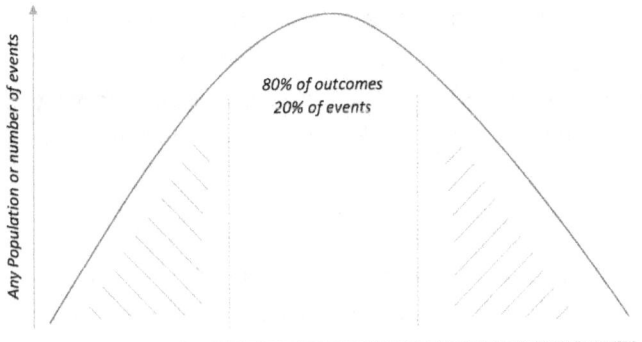

The perfectionists out there are going to hate this principle – but consider that 80:20 doesn't mean stopping short. It just requires you to think about where effort is useful and necessary and not simply busy work.

You can use 80:20 to pick your battles. Consider this: A Promoter[7] type sets the vision, sounds the battle cry then leads the charge, but 20% into the campaign, he or she begins to flag, hankering instead for the next big thing. 80% of her dopamine has been delivered. The rush has gone and the thrill of the chase is over just 20% into the campaign.

Repeated hits of dopamine can help her traverse the long 80% to come – at least better than a cattle prod. Perhaps she can bring in a Controller to

---

[7] You can read about Operating Modes in Volume 1

take the reins for the long road ahead – it's the sort of road that suits those types well.

Realize also that applying the 80:20 Pareto principle to everything does mean *many* things are simply not going to get attention when all's working well. Learn that that's okay if the big things *are* happening.

Cutting things which aren't working is one of the best uses of Pareto. Sometimes it pays to leave things incomplete, unresolved and unfinished so you are much less attached when the cull comes.

Remember that outstanding people are rarely if ever known for more than one achievement in their lifetime, even if they had been working on 3-5. This is the 80:20 Pareto principle at work. Their crowning achievement will usually have come from perhaps just 1/5 of their effort.

How many people have read JK Rowling's wider range of novels – not just *Harry Potter*? Who knows that *Indiana Jones* was George Lucas' idea? All he did was Star Wars, wasn't it?

The rest shouldn't be seen as waste, however, if it was clearly enjoyed, designed to mitigate risk or to learn something transferable into their main arena.

A final word: Stay focused on whatever is great for your Résumé. You can't be promoted or get a job for being great at inbox clearing (though that can be useful for PR, if nothing else). Many coachees tell me they're busy all day but can't point to what they've achieved by the end of the week. That's because they're often just doing busy stuff which is easily forgettable and has nothing to show for itself.

Strategy #22: Know Your Key Success Factors

How do you determine what's important?

It sounds like a silly question, but amongst the myriad things coming at you, it can feel surprisingly difficult to be sure at times.

We're looking for *great* stuff, not merely *good* stuff. That's tough, whereas sorting the good from the bad is relatively easy for most of us.

You don't want to forego great opportunities which may never return.

Think of things which have an obviously large benefit (B) or large potential for loss (L). We looked at this above with the Eisenhower matrix. Things to consider are not just financial but could include lifestyle, heritage, reputation and so on.

Do you really know what's critical to doing your job well? I mean *really* know? Sometimes it can be obscure. Is it to check off *everything* on your To Do? That's unlikely, but I'll bet that's where you focus much of your attention. So don't operate that way.

Understand the distinction between hygiene factors and success factors. The former gets you in the

race (so to speak). It's the latter that's the difference between winning or losing and making an impact.

A runner needs decent shoes – hygiene factor. A functional head needs technical knowledge of his or her business – hygiene factor. Both also need bulletproof mental and interaction strategies – success factor.

In one of my corporate roles, there were two de-facto models of success for my grade. One was to deliver large projects over one to several years, technically known as tending the farm – a farm which others had largely planted before me. If you've read Volume 1 of the series, you may recognize this as a *Caretaker* or *Controller* mode of operating. The other part of my role was to build a portfolio of new clients, otherwise known as hunting. From Volume 1, you'll know this as a *promoter* mode of operating.

It's generally easier to farm than to hunt, because in the former you're essentially jumping onto someone else's bandwagon and leveraging technical knowledge gleaned over decades. Don't get me wrong – that's good if you can do it well. But it's not *great*.

Building a new client portfolio and mastering a new solution to common problems was the unsaid definition of *great* in that business. My mode of operation, therefore, was to mix farming with hunting and that had real impact and even influenced the role description for my peers thereafter. That was all within the first year of the position.

To understanding what impact really means, go beyond doing what you're told or whatever's written in your role description. Impactful people play the game – then change it for the better.

Questions

1. Using the 80:20 rule in the previous strategy, where could you better focus your energies? ....

2. What are the key success factors in your role? ....

Strategy #23: Trust the Process

We've already said that vision can be engaging but doesn't deliver anything in of itself. Though vision gives rise to dreams, it's equally adept at delivering illusions, broken promises and disillusionment.

Productivity, however, is the *only* thing that delivers results.

You'll succeed (or fail) in your priorities by implementing a good process (or not) and sticking to it (or not).

The process may be a systematic way of doing things. It could be a habit, a routine or a ritual. It could be a decision tree. Design a good process and follow it.

Impact is in the doing, not the dreaming.

Question

1. What's the day-by-day repeatable process by which you get your activities done? ....

Strategy #24: Make Winning Decisions and Choices

It's been said that we're doomed to simply make choices (for choices, read decisions).

A lot of the strategies we've already covered are about first choosing to spend your time where you'll have the most impact.

So, the decisions and choices you make will send you either up a ladder or down a snake's back. Learn how to make good choices.

We're derailed by our humanity and perceptions of right and wrong when it comes to making consistently good decisions. When the stakes get bigger, decisions often feel more like dilemmas and you may feel indecisive where once you were quick and clear. This is often called brain fog.

Once you evolve beyond your basic needs for food, shelter, career, reputation and so on – or if you've argued for freedom and gained it – your mind will be freed to cogitate over free choice. But it's scary when you can't handle freedom.

Rudderless or free falling for the first time, you may have unanswerable questions. You may look back towards the certainty you once knew, feeling unable to choose the constraints that gave that certainty in the first place. This becomes a bigger challenge the higher up the ladder you go. So, what do you do? How do you make good decisions while avoiding all the natural biases we all carry around?

We help ourselves by having a good process that also gives a sense of direction.

First, recognize that decisions, particularly difficult ones, are really trade-offs rather than rights or wrongs.

What you settle for now, may well be appropriate for now, but not necessarily a clear-cut best choice overall for all time.

Second, be aware of the biases just off stage. We talked about some of these in Volume 1.

Off-stage Decision Influencers[8]

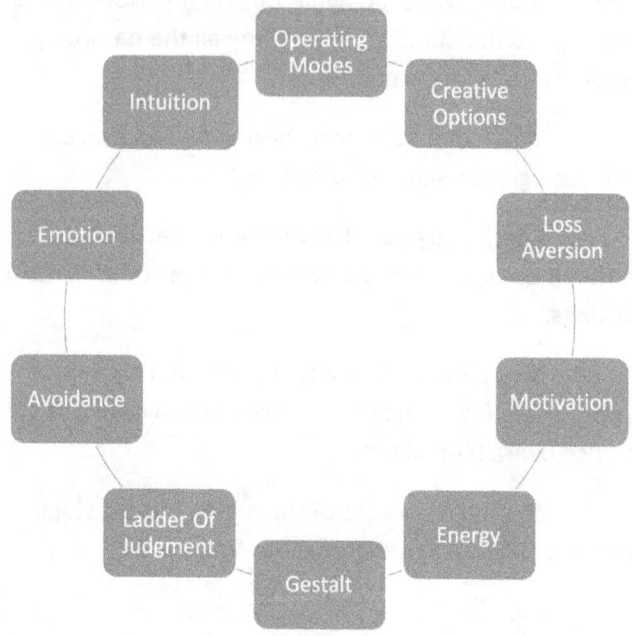

We now draw upon several of the strategies from Volume 1 of the series to explain the myriad of factors that can unduly influence decisions:

- **Operating Modes**: If you're an Analyzer and to some extent a Controller too, you're probably the type of person who likes to make the *best* decision whenever faced with a choice.

---

[8] See Volume 1 for more detail on these influencers

My advice would be to leave wriggle room in your options and outcomes. There's no such thing as a *perfect* decision, but wriggle room will give you space for further analysis to satisfy your need to try and find one. You will also avoid regret from getting locked into the *wrong* choice with hindsight.

You might also learn to accept and trade small losses for bigger gains.

If, on the other hand, you can't make decisions given half a choice, it may be best to get help to narrow your options quickly.

This can even be artificial narrowing until you have no choice at all! You may not make the best choice, so it's usually best to move on quickly and accept that Analyzers and Controllers will likely trump your decisions whenever the stakes really count.

- **Creative Options:** Robust decisions arise from good options. Where you don't have options, you have foregone conclusions; you essentially walk straight into someone's agenda.

Get creative and think of combinations and packages of different outcomes. Dream up the unthinkable.

The aim at the beginning of a decision is to count options in – not out.

Work hard to create at least two, better still three, equally good options to make you indifferent to any one of them going bad. It's a strategy which dampens short-term emotion and subverts our all-powerful loss aversion. It also prevents you from thinking *either/or*, and gets you thinking *both,* wherever that's possible.

- **Loss Aversion**. In a decision, you're usually giving up something in order to get something else – perhaps something bigger and better. That's the tradeoff.

When you find it difficult to let go of that something – usually something you own – ask yourself what you will gain from doing so.

This offsets a natural tendency to only think of the downsides in a trade or decision. You'll find that a loss can be acceptable if offset by a bigger benefit.

Understand and shore up potential pitfalls and downsides.

Have a strategy in case things go south so that your choices and decisions are not hijacked by loss aversion.

Be prepared by knowing in advance when you'll have to cut loose then stick to that rule if the time comes.

Finally, avoid reacting when there's a high chance of forced error and no way to back out.

- **Motivation:** Understand your motivations and how your different options serve them.

    Be aware of how your motivations unduly favor certain outcomes and foregone conclusions that aren't in your best interest in the moment. You can read more about these in Volume 1.

- **Manage your energy:** Avoid draining your reserves by repeatedly making decisions about repeated decisions and choices (repetition is tedious, isn't it)?

    Apply rules, also known as 'If This, Then That', for repeated events.

    Things which are important should happen on autopilot. Try running[9] when making difficult decisions – it frees you from mental shackles.

    When you're tired, you'll make poor decisions. It's always easier to take the easy option.

- **Gestalt:** We looked at this in Volume 1. Basically, it's the need for closure and the ability to see patterns which aren't necessarily there.

    There's an old adage that *any decision is better than no decision.* This sounds a lot like wanting closure or resolution for its own sake (see Volume 1 for more

---

[9] Try running when you have big decisions to make. This trick keeps your brain just a little too busy for short-term emotion and frees you to think more objectively. Movement also lifts your mental anchor, so in a sense, you're getting out of your own head with every step.

on Gestalt). I don't subscribe to that, unless the stakes are inconsequential.

My own view is that no decision is better than a regretful decision. Don't make unnecessary decisions just to feel complete or fill a void.

You don't want short term emotion pulling the wrong strings. Perhaps your action can wait for the right moment. With a reaction, you may seem in control to the unwary, but that isn't in itself a feature of a good decision.

Gestalt also drives us to focus on closure over gain. We don't want loose ends, however inconsequential they may be (perhaps this is evolutionary: something might come back to bite). This drives the incessant ticking off of To-Dos items of little benefit, whereas we'd be better off accepting open loops, and focusing instead on bigger gains elsewhere. If you're a Controller, look for activities which move the needle the most in your priorities, then actively choose to leave undone any inconsequential minutiae. Remember, you get more of whatever you focus on.

- **Ladder of Judgment:** Again, we covered this in Volume 1. Remember, we tend to see only what we're already looking for. That means you need to get the full picture to avoid what's known as a confirmation bias.

Good decisions rely on good information, so get the information you need, even if it requires more time.

Remember to also look for evidence to challenge your pre-conceived ideas – such evidence usually sits off-stage and is easy to ignore. Accept it for what it is. The way to achieve this is to incorporate diversity and *invite* challenge to conventional thinking.

Avoid automatically trusting your gut unless you're in personally familiar territory, which is highly repeatable and predictable too.

Make your decision more like a rule, more than a decision.

Try stepping out of your own head and pretend to advise a friend in your shoes, as if you're making decisions from afar.

- **If you're not making choices, someone else is.** Life, and work are a set of choices.

What project? Which company? How much? By when? and so on. But it gets broader. Someone chooses what jobs are open for application, what work you'll be doing, how you should dress, your work hours, and so on and so on. We seem to be remarkably controlled, with just an illusion of free choice. But is that really the case?

Many young professionals fail to negotiate choices, fearful that they don't have a right. But that is a choice too.

No choice is a choice.

We always have a choice, and sometimes our choice may not win the day. That's okay. Treat choice as a set of tradeoffs, options and negotiations.

- **Emotion.** We are emotionally driven, veiled by the illusion of rationality. We like to think that we make decisions rationally, but a lot of research shows that we, in-fact, make them emotionally and simply create rational explanations (for ourselves as much others). We are at heart story telling creatures.

But emotions – particularly short-term emotions – often derail good decisions. Short-term emotions often put us in fight or flight mode and our inbuilt reactions work to protect us from danger, even when it's imagined and there isn't any immediate threat.

Emotion blurs your thinking, so that all your energy can be redirected towards self-protection in a highly charged situation.

Learn to recognize and back off from especially tricky situations, so that short-term emotions can pass.

Once that's happened, you will be better equipped to face situations logically and analytically. How long to back off? It depends on you; sometimes minutes, other times hours, days or even weeks. The term 'sleep on it' comes to mind as you often wake up with a cleaner slate. Simply allow yourself the time to calm down and find perspective. If you can see and accept other perspectives, as well as your own, that's probably a good sign that your head's back to where it should be.

- **Intuition**. We like decisions to be easy and prefer outcomes which fit our worldview. Thinking, however, can be exhausting and will often throw up unwelcome challenges to what we expect or want to see.

So, we use intuition as a mental shortcut instead, using patterns from the past to make judgements about the present and future. Intuition leans on the amygdala, a part of the more primitive mid-brain which is horribly poor at computing probabilities and outcomes objectively. It relies instead on whatever's top of mind or more recent in memory than what came before, or might be more relevant or significant. The primitive parts of the brain are also self-centered and highly subjective.

The good news, however, is that intuition is dependable when we're dealing with highly repeatable patterns within our control. Outside of *that* realm, intuition begins to fail fast for all the reasons above.

The last thing our brains want is to be *wrong*, so they create and fill in plausible stories in order 'to be right,' which is one of the reasons why intuition can be so derailing. We're simply not conscious of that story writing in the background and don't reject our intuition enough because the result is often comfortable and at least plausible – even if fictional.

So how do we make the most of the merits of intuition? It's best to slow down and listen to what your gut says without committing quickly or impulsively to a course of action. This acknowledges elements of your past experience, while also allowing space and time for some mental challenge to the ideas thrown up. Slowing down creates room for broader inputs and provides the opportunity for the frontal cortex to fire up and join in the challenge of making good decisions.

So, you can see that a key sign of good decisions, therefore, is good process.

Accept that it will be a lengthy process sometimes.

Good decisions take time and work, and they are rarely the result of gut feel.

When you don't see process in a corporate setting, you have the clearest sign that you're being set up for a foregone conclusion or agenda.

Knowing all that, how do you get others to make the decisions that you want? A number of strategies can help:

- Understand 'what's in it' for the decision maker? You *have to* tap into their self-centered mid-brain.
- Crystallize the change from a decision (or indecision), by showing clear benefits or losses. Make it clear what exactly the decision maker is choosing e.g. the before versus after that we've all seen in ads for weight loss products.
- Avoid having your decision makers do the thinking if you want them to make a choice easily. What'll happen is that they'll avoid the thinking and, as a result, the decision too!
- Use story telling. We all remember beginnings and ends and respond to being shown things, rather than told about them. Tell a good story and make it emotional to tap into the amygdala, using anxiety, anger, awe or sadness to leverage natural loss aversion and drive quick action. You should also highlight benefits, perhaps embracing a vision. We'll delve deeper into story-telling in Volume 3.
- If you're after a *big* decision, use incremental steps rather than a big bang. You'll be leveraging the natural consistency bias which leads us to act consistently with prior small steps in the right direction.

Questions

1. Which of the above factors most often undermine your choices or decisions? ....

2. How will you remain more aware of them (perhaps reviewing the items regularly, when making decisions)? ...

Summary A

Okay, so that completes the first part of our productivity circle – triage.

We leant about the why and the how of triage using the Eisenhower matrix. We then looked at picking out our top 1-3 priorities and finding the 80:20 rule in all that we do. We thought about our key success factors and how they differ from the hygiene factors. Finally, we put our faith in process and learnt to make winning decisions.

All of that is aimed at helping you make the right choices over whatever it is that you do.

If you do triage well, you'll be left with a set of priorities which have made it through the bullshit filter.

B. Habit and Routine

Good habits and routine push important things out of reach of indecision.

We're plagued by indecision continually.

The idea here is to defend the time allocated specifically to whatever's supremely important, and to make it as easy as possible for you *to show up* each and every time. It's the realm of autopilot.

Habits and rituals lower the energy requirement to get things done. When you keep plates spinning, you won't have to waste energy fighting inertia to start them up over and over again.

Tiny steps lead the way for big ones. Pretty quickly, your consistency bias kicks in and you start to feel compelled to continue with the habits you've formed.

Rituals, particularly, are the preserve of top athletes and elite musicians – followed specifically to prepare the mind and body for performance.

If you start the day trying to decide whether or not to do something important, you've already begun working against yourself. Obvious examples might be practicing an instrument, daily exercise, or even regular nurturing of your work network. It's always easier to find an excuse and say 'tomorrow.'

Habit and routine prevent this from happening, without you having to try too hard.

But remember, habits are best when purposed to achieving specific goals (the goals you set in Mode A), otherwise they're just treadmills to nowhere.

How long does it take to form a habit? There are numbers floating around like twenty-one days, eighteen to two hundred and fifty days and so on, but the truth is that it depends upon the amount of focused effort you're willing to put in at the start.

A habit could be instant with a decision to do something a certain way from now on, or it could cement slowly over a short period as you persist daily with whatever you've decided to do. The basal ganglia part of the brain then will take over, freeing your frontal cortex to focus elsewhere. This is why it becomes progressively easier to live with an ingrained habit over time. What we've done with habit, then, is to lower the energy required to do things in a certain way consistently.

Strategy #25: Avoid Willpower. Consistency is King

Did you know that consistency, creativity and time are enough to conquer all territory? To allow eventual domination of any domain (assuming sufficiently deep pockets)?

It takes sustained effort to create something with impact. Humanity's had eons – before you were even a good idea – to figure out how things should be. You're playing catch-up. How do you catch-up? By putting in sustained effort.

Avoid reliance on mystical willpower – that's equivalent to pushing snowballs uphill.

Rely instead on habit and routine. They bring their own slow-burn energy.

Remember the top half of your triage chart? The important things? Build habits and *good* morning routines for those things.

I'll give you two good reasons for doing this:

1. The important things will become automatic. This takes the pain out of anything which requires sustained effort over a long period.

2. You'll get a daily psychological boost from progressing or completing important things first and before the day moves in. The rest of the day can even be filled with crud, though you'll find that it won't matter quite so much.

Try to make habits daily, because interruption – even one day – results in non-habit. A famous violinist once said, *When I don't practice one day – I notice. When I miss two days – my wife notices. Three days, and everyone knows!*

If you allow inertia, doubt, indecision, choice, negotiation and so on to creep in between you and what you want to achieve, you'll make things more difficult for yourself.

You've read about the many ways in which you and the world derail you every day – so don't willingly give ground.

I've personally shunned habit for most of my life, mainly because it felt boring. You too may find that things get dull once you've settled into a habit, even if it's working perfectly for you.

That boredom undermines you, so you'll begin to look for distractions. This is natural, because we are all experience-seeking creatures. This is the mental mechanism which keeps our primeval pattern-recognition capabilities well-oiled and working.

But habit, in a sense, also keeps us glued to a spot in order to maintain, or to shore up, something important – call it a defensive approach, or *caretaking.*

Experience-seeking, however, drives us to find new stories to add to our own – call it an offensive approach, or *promoting*.

If you understood your prevalent operating mode from Volume 1, you'll see how easy or difficult it may be to maintain habits. Promoters thrive on spontaneity, whereas Controllers tread water with predictability.

If you're **highly habitual** (perhaps a natural Controller or Caretaker type):

- Allow yourself the freedom to find and experience new things to add spice to your routine.

You might want to inject more diversity into your work. While habits and routine are useful, beware of being blinded by a compulsion to remain consistent with your commitments – others can use that trait against you, for instance by having you work on something you really ought not to be working on, or perhaps requesting long hours of you or concessions on your time. You might find yourself self-rationalizing why long hours are even necessary, or good, supporting an unhelpful cause.

The best way to overcome this compulsion is to ensure that exceptions aren't allowed to evolve quietly into rules, habits and routines.

If you're **highly spontaneous** and constantly distracted:

- You're perhaps unable to sit still. Try to focus on implementing just one or two habits for the truly important things, and let those embed first, before adding another
- You could think about getting to work early to tackle a specific daily task, or triaging your activities every evening.

Congratulations! Simply combining the *connecting* strategies in Volume 1 with the triage and habits strategies in Volume 2, you're now acting like the top 3-4% of impactful people the world over.

Strategy #26: You Have No choice

Having argued for making our own choices, I'm now going to suggest that you kill your choices.

You may have heard about the paradox of choice. Put simply, a lot of choice befuddles us, leaving us dissatisfied when we do make one. Freedom isn't as good as it's made out to be and humans are not that good at it.

What's behind this? It's rarely possible to make a perfect choice about anything. We get brain fog and end up feeling at least some regret in *every* decision.

Understand that the paradox of choice applies to how you spend your time. We know that important things *shouldn't* require frequent decisions for implementation – they are important after all, are they not?

What we need, therefore, is to avoid having to make the same choices repeatedly over how we spend our time.

First, let's simply have fewer choices – or even no choice at all. Choice demands decisions and decisions consume energy; but unnecessary decisions are wasteful of energy. That's where habit and routine comes in.

You can kick start that process easily too. As an example, I used to travel a lot for work and often returned to a hotel in the evening with a mountain of things to do. I was training for a marathon and learning to play violin, whilst also writing a novel. I liked to FaceTime my family, scan the news on a range of topics, go to dinner or bars with colleagues and so on. How could I possibly do all this each evening? Well, I couldn't. I could wing it day by day, but I knew I'd look back with regret at time spent badly, and at the very least in overwhelm – and in my own time too!

I decided to give myself little or no choice. I could EITHER sit quietly (off the bed, without TV or internet), OR choose to do ONE of violin, running or write my novel – that's after my family call. Though sitting quietly wasn't punishment, five minutes into staring out the window or at the walls, the violin or running shoes invariably came out. After dinner, I'd write some words in the book.

All I had really done was use the paradox of choice to rule out unhelpful choices in the moment.

When you think about your one thing each and every morning, this is essentially what you're doing, to give yourself clarity to do what's most important. You're also recognizing choice as a tradeoff – you sometimes incur a small loss, to gain big elsewhere.

Strategy #27: Be Grateful on Cue Each Day

Have you noticed how habitually negative you are?

Being fearful or anxious also seems to require no effort at all. It's contagious and affects your performance in everything you do, and in the relationships you rely on.

Being grateful, however, builds empathy, understanding and authenticity, all of which are essential for creating a connection to others.

If you've read Volume 1, you'll know how essential connection is for impact. If you go on to read Volume 3, you'll read how important authenticity is for building trust in communication.

But there's more. Being grateful is a state in which you are more *conscious* – that is, fully aware and using the frontal cortex to make good choices. In a nutshell, it keeps you present.

Conversely, when you're anxious or disappointed, your subconscious weighs in more heavily to protect you from perceived threats.

It's more emotional and simply not competent at weighing up choice objectively, beyond removing you from imagined dangers. It doesn't necessarily see those imagined dangers as the seed of opportunity. That, instead, requires at least half a rational thought.

Have you ever noticed how remaining positive in the face of challenges is – well, challenging? Staying positive can be elusive, whereas negativity seems to take care of itself.

Remember, your head is loss averse, hence quite heavily negatively biased. Negativity is way easier to spread – and catch – simply because our subconscious weighs it heavily to stay top of mind; and whatever's top of mind dominates the subconscious. Paradoxically, this is the success story of evolution – we're still here, after all!

As an example, think about your last performance appraisal. It was all good, until your boss dropped one smallish thing that you could improve on. What do you dwell on? If you're like the rest of humanity, you dwell on the smallish negative as if it filled the room. Is that a balanced perspective? I think you'll agree that it's not.

Remaining positive takes work. It requires a constant input of energy, but you can make it much easier by using the power of habit.

Here's how:

- At the beginning or end of the day, think about all the positives, and the things which weren't quite as bad as you expected during the previous day. You

can do this at the dinner table, in the shower or wherever you are. Tie it to a regular environment or activity to trigger the habitual thought process
- Reel off as many of these items as you can. Size doesn't matter, for your subconscious can't tell the difference between big and small. Fact or fiction doesn't matter either – again, your subconscious can't tell one from the other. Aim for a surprisingly good number of items
- Bask in the glow of one or more of your items, or on the size of your list
- Manufacture the feeling of winning by acknowledging small but meaningful advances. It's our default to overlook progress towards big goals, mainly because incremental advances are dwarfed by the big kahuna itself. This strategy may even singularly keep you on a path where others have bailed out with their own limiting beliefs, which dominate their thoughts. So, make it a deliberate practice.
- When you're disheartened about something that isn't working in the way you intended, figure out what it is that you want and write it down. This engages the frontal cortex, which behaves rationally and objectively, calming the amygdala. Then keep at it. You could also place yourself in a position of perspective and pretend to advice a friend standing in your shoes. We wrote more about these when we looked at behavior in Volume 1.
- Acknowledge that we're not necessarily wired to feel positive. Our brains instead seek out patterns which might represent problems or danger.

Additionally, feeling good about one area of your work is often at the expense of others in your life. For instance, throwing hours at office success is almost certain to be at the expense of sleep, your social and personal life – and vice versa.

Nevertheless, what you'll quickly realize is that even on a bad day (from a poor perspective), you still have a dozen or more things to be grateful for.

What you're doing here is cultivating a helpful and habitual way of thinking. You're routinely tackling the brain's tendency to look for losses, risks and downsides which naturally dominate your thinking, even though not actually warranted most of the time.

Whatever you do, you'll get more of whatever you focus on.

So, keep your head balanced, preserving your energy for impact tomorrow.

Questions

Now answer these questions on habit and routine.

1. What from your priorities would benefit most from a daily habit or routine? ....
2. What will your routine or habit look like and what will trigger it (place, person, etc)? ....
3. When are you routinely most prone to making poor choice? ....
4. How can you help yourself by eliminating options (for Promoters), or leaving open options (for Controllers) while accepting loss of choice or control? ....
5. When and where will you be routinely grateful each day? .

Summary B

Okay, so that completes the second part of our productivity circle – habit and routine.

We learnt about the why habit and routine are way more powerful than willpower to accomplish what's important. We then learnt to routinely restrict our choices in order to narrow our attention onto those important choices we have to make. Finally, we learnt to be grateful each day, to remind ourselves about the progress we make on what's important to us and feel it.

All of that is aimed at helping you make the most of what's important, automatically.

If you have good habits and routines, you'll be streets ahead of the pack in achieving something with meaningful impact.

C. Batching

The idea behind batching is quite simply about boosting efficiency. How do you allocate your mental and physical effort for maximum effect and avoid unnecessary duplication and repetition?

Look for batching opportunities in whatever you do and you will accomplish everything with much less time and energy.

This is another way of lowering the bar. When you batch, you're using the power of muscle memory to add momentum to your activity.

There are other tangible benefits too.

Batching of the important improves your recall of what you did, whereas batching of crud boxes it in and prevents it from sucking the life out of you.

We want to prevent crud piling on top like ash from a volcano and smothering any life that's underneath.

As an example, imagine that you're writing a report. You might batch the research first, all the writing next and then batch-process feedback in one shot, right at the end. Make all your calls in a batch. That way of working's a lot more efficient than doing each task several times over and over each day, as you push the report along.

When you're *not* batching, you are in fact task switching, or multi-tasking, both of which are highly inefficient.

In switching mode, you're repeatedly thrown out of an otherwise engaging activity, so you're much less likely to get into a flow state or even recall what each engagement entailed. We'll discuss this more in the multi-tasking myth.

Luckily, many things we do, day to day, can be batched in some fashion and you probably already do it without realizing. Try to push this principle more and more in all that you do.

You have to look for ways of breaking down an activity into constituent parts. For example, publishing a paper consists of writing, reviewing, processing feedback, production and publishing. It may make sense to write several documents together, have a review period for all, process all the feedback in one shot, then produce and publish them together. In a non-batched process, you'd repeat the cycle one paper at a time. That's inefficient.

Strategy #28: Don't Manage Email

Email, particularly, has become an epic problem at work. We send 108 billion emails a day and it swallows up to a quarter of our time being unproductive. It's become such a nemesis that many of us feel compelled to clear our work inbox when we're on vacation, so that we don't return to a mountain of messages. The French government has gone so far as looking for ways to give employees the right to disconnect during their own time and some organizations have already experimented with doing away with email altogether. French IT firm Atos Origin began ditching it several years ago, believing it sucked the life out of employee productivity. Even at home, signing up for anything online seems to bring a flood of unwanted sales communication wearing out the delete button on the keyboard.

People have postulated all sort of techniques to dealing with email, including zero inboxing, wiping the inbox clean periodically, filtering, filing, searching and so on and so on. It's become such an epic problem that apps now use VIP labels to filter out almost everything we get. But productivity apps just allow you to squeeze more of it in. The problem is that, when technology's there to hold the door open to your attention – round the clock – you don't humanly stand a chance. Forget it about managing it.

Some organizations have even suggested replacing email with…well, instant messages. It's clearly a problem!

And social media's potentially worse. While email clients allow filtering, professional network, LinkedIn, recently removed this feature and the other networks fare no better. Now there's simply no way to filter the signal from the bottomless pit of noise. The best you can do is unfollow incessant posters.

My suggestion is that you don't waste a second managing email or social media, but stay focused on your priorities, treating email as another signal – or noise, if you prefer. Understand that email and messaging are glorified To-Do lists which the rest of the world tops-up for you.

They are modern-day treadmills and it's folly to believe you can be in control. So what's the best solution and why the rant?

Well, email takes up most of our working lives yet, sadly, we crank out emails a lot more than meaningful outcomes from our time – outcomes we can hold up with pride. Most of us suffer email overload almost continuously and research shows employees are happier and more productive when they are shot of it at work, because the less control they have over time, the more they suffer from time pressure.

Luckily, email is a sitting duck for triage and batch processing:

1) First, deflect incoming messages with automated filters and rules that automatically place emails into folders (including trash). Gmail and iCloud have these, as does Outlook. You will batch review these folders at a convenient time i.e. read, ignore or delete. In some email systems, trash is automatically deleted after 30 days, so you have ample chance to look at something if it's important. If not, you've just eliminated a whole bunch of processing
2) At the start of your day, scan your inbox to check if there are any fires you may need to put out. Think hard about what genuinely needs processing as a priority versus what can wait.
3) As you go about your day, your head should be in your triage system and focused on your priorities, not your email. Access email when required for one of your priorities. Give yourself a time limit then dip into the appropriate email folder twice or thrice daily (or every few hours on projects where email seems to be the main deliverable)!
4) Triage anything that's in the inbox and not automatically re-directed to an appropriate folder. Do this without reading it – it can wait for your attention. One of your folders should be an Important Urgent mailbox (have a look at the Eisenhower matrix at the start of this book) – go there first and deal with anything urgent now

5) Don't reply to email immediately unless you want to start a conversation. You can prevent email overload by...not sending any, or timing replies to slow down the process.
6) Send what you need to a printer if you must, so you can disconnect from your inbox quickly and when reading is all you're really after. Close your email
7) Every few days or once a week, batch read or clear out folders according to your priorities, unsubscribing from anything that always gets delete treatment
8) If you're running a project that generates a lot of email, batch the team communication into daily meetings to cut down on email traffic.

One of the reasons why this is so effective is that it keeps you in a position of perspective.

When you have everything laid out in front of you e.g. a folder with a batch of emails about a project, it's much easier to avoid what's not important within your limited time.

The items at the bottom of the list stay at the bottom and you naturally and easily prioritize your time to what's genuinely worthwhile and high priority. That's where you have impact.

You also remain focused and use energy efficiently. Processing every email as it comes in has a painfully high task-switching cost. Since the 80:20 Pareto principle is at work, you will expend energy on the unimportant.

Batching, though, means dipping in and out fewer times and on purpose. A similar task may have cropped up three separate times, but with the benefit of perspective, you can combine and tackle them together in one shot. That's efficient.

With batching, you're also utilizing the power of flow, whilst kicking repeated opportunity for inertia in the butt.

Transition between tasks can be wasteful, whereas flow is productive. Flow makes everything feel easy and enjoyable.

Out of sight is literally out of mind. The brain, unfortunately, can't ignore what's in front of it (try looking at any advert and not reading the words. You can't). The brain's also highly distractible (try ignoring the dings on your smartphone for a day. You can't). Filtering email means your attention won't be hijacked for someone else's purpose in the moment.

Smartphones with email and messages clearly present a big challenge. Email's convenient when you want it, but also highly inconvenient the next moment when it interrupts. The best advice is to turn off notifications and actively *decide* when to pick up your phone to check your email. The best moments are surely when you can act on whatever needs doing in one go.

Try putting your smartphone away for short periods of say 10-20 minutes during the day. Build up

that time and eventually switch back to a good old dumb phone.

Basic product marketing psychology is at work against you – frequent touch drives product stickiness. Avoidance and abstinence are the easiest failsafe ways to prevent unwanted distraction.

Questions

1. In which of your activities are you most likely to benefit from batching e.g. communication, document processing, travel, etc? ....

2. How and when will you implement the batching routine?

Summary C

That completes the third part of our productivity circle – batching.

We learnt how batching makes everything more efficient and gives you much needed perspective over all the commitments in front of you. We used email as an example of how and why to batch activities.

If you do batching well, you'll be much more efficient and focused than the rest of the pack.

D. Airplane Mode

Some people call this going dark.

The idea behind focus is to close the door on the world and avoid distraction and interruption like the plague. You're closing the door because you've learnt that your brain is a distraction magnet – we already read that it scans for patterns in whatever's going on around us, searching for changes which could represent danger. A study on an eight-year-old who suffered a head injury back in the 1950s, revealed a phenomenon called blind sight, which demonstrated that we subconsciously *see* (are aware of) what we're not consciously attentive to. You probably know the feeling that something's not quite right, even if you don't know specifically what's out of kilter.

So, you can probably tell from what you've read, then, that I'm a big believer in creating the right environment for effective focus. This is the prime purpose of airplane mode in the productivity cycle.

Having the right environment is yet another way to make it easier for you to get on with something notable (though it may be hard). It's like escaping gravity by using only a fraction of the energy normally required.

When you're doing the doing and you have filtered out the 80% of noise, you're going to spend all your time in the trenches – in the weeds – simply because you love what you're doing. In this mode, you leave nothing to chance.

What you focus on *is* you. When you're *doing*, your aim is to withdraw energy from the outside world and re-focus it on the task at hand. You're trying to avoid distraction for specific amounts of time.

It could be for 30-minute intervals throughout the day, half a day each day or even several days at a time. Creatives will often disappear for months at a time. Sir Isaac Newton even disappeared for years, only to reappear from seclusion with the greatest discoveries in mathematics and physics of all time. Even Hitler would disappear at times to avoid his motives being *positively* influenced!

How much time do you need? Whatever's necessary to stay focused, engaged and productive. There's a common perception that you need to spend 10,000 hours on something for mastery. Whether true or not, focus will get you there much quicker.

Okay, so you're now breathing rarified air and learning from the top 1% of impactful people.

Now go do the work. This is where it all happens. You're at the top of your particular tree.

Here are some strategies to help you:

- **Decide to tackle just on one item of necessary crud per day.** Just one per day, so you're not climbing a mountain of crud by the end of the week. Remember our definition of crud is anything that won't stand as an accolade on your tombstone. At work, it's anything you can't put in your Résumé or

talk about at your next job or promotion interview. (But you also don't want to talk about why you were fired for not doing it)
- **Think of your days as two halves**, and focus the first half on one of your important items, the second on another. Chunking into smaller time slots of say 30 minutes or 1 hour is not productive. It's best applied only to necessary crud like meetings you'd rather not attend, chaser calls and other corporate process
- **Set a short timer for the things that normally swallow your time** like expenses, email, smartphones, social media, browsing, etc. Try and sprint your way through these
- Theme your weeks for different elements of your role or projects. That'll give you sufficient time to get into them
- **Focus only on what you do control** and be brutally honest about where that span of control stops. Don't get attached to outcomes that are not in your power to determine
- **Simple always works best** (unless you're *selling* financial services!). Simple has an unbeatable elegance. Why? In Volume 1, we talked about the Ladder of Inference, and our bias towards trusting more in less. *Simple* suggests essence and therefore feels genuine. It takes less cognitive effort to engage in simple, so it's always preferred over complex. Simple also suggests something will *work in all weathers*. The less you give people *reason* to think, the more likely they are to go with whatever you're saying. This is marketing 101

- **Aim high, and at worst you might produce something mediocre.** Also remember, if you're working to a budget (time or money) you're almost certain to low-ball what's actually possible. That's because quality takes time and a lot of iteration. Creating something new is always subject to a planning fallacy (a low-balling bias), unknown unknowns and optimism bias, so you're almost certain to need more than first expected
- **Don't worry too much about outcomes – focus on inputs**, because that's what you control. Make intent, commitment, integrity, support – and hours – count, because an outcome may not be as motivating as it once seemed when you finally get there
- **Leverage scarcity,** by not responding immediately to requests. The sender, seeking Gestalt in your response, will run after you, while scarcity will enhance your perceived value

Strategy #29: Find Focus with Pomodoro, and Avoid Distraction with Internet Blockers

We've already talked about distraction and you've probably surmised by now that it cannot be overcome easily with willpower.

As a strategy, willpower's an uphill struggle because we're wired to be distractible. You're attuned to movement lurking in the darkness or just beyond reach, so you'd be utilizing mental energy to defeat your DNA. Secret: DNA's been winning for eons. You'd be chasing your tail.

So, now in the productivity cycle, we physically remove ourselves from the source of distraction completely, whenever we can. We close the door on the world, get noise cancelling headphones or whatever.

Computers and smartphones are built as distraction machines as much as productivity tools, because their economic value is generally based in their habit forming potential. The more we're conditioned to look at the shiny objects or notification updates, the more our personal resistance to distraction can diminish, suggests research. When we repeatedly look for notifications, we habitually reinforce our own inability to focus. And this is clearly a problem, because there are even apps on the very same devices which help us to tune out and find focus again:

- *Focus Booster[10]*. This is a simple Pomodoro timer which dings anywhere between 20-45 minutes of focus. You'd then take a 5-10 minutes break to rejuvenate your brain's glucose store. Studies show you can maintain your creativity during a break by doing different low-level cognitive tasks. Switching off completely allows inertia to creep in
- *Anti-social[11]*. As it says, this turns off websites and social networks at your choosing
- *Freedom[12]* will disconnect your internet connection for hours at a time
- *SelfControl[13]* for Mac turns off websites, email or anything internet, for however long you want
- *Cold Turkey[14]* promises fewer distractions and more free time, blocking internet and schedule pop ups.

If dinging devices are your problem, avoid treating all notifications on your devices equally. Try not to have them all in one place all vying for your attention concurrently. Avoid leaving desktop tabs open and clear out anything from your desktop that you don't regularly use. Avoid looking at your phone first thing in the day,

---

[10] Focus Booster http://download.cnet.com/Focus-Booster/3000-2350_4-10971798.html
[11] Anti-social http://anti-social.cc/
[12] Freedom https://freedom.to/
[13] SelfControl http://selfcontrolapp.com/
[14] Cold Turkey http://getcoldturkey.com/

then increase that gap one step at a time until you find your ability to focus again.

These are some of the ways in which *the insignificant* sneaks in on the coat tails of the important. These are the easiest ways to have your attention scattered every time you dip in – remember out of sight is literally out of mind.

The world never ended because someone had to wait a little longer for attention.

Questions

1. Which electronic distractions will you disconnect from during focus time? ....

2. Which apps might be helpful? ....

Strategy #30: Remain Present to Focus On What's in Front of You

Negativity depends almost entirely on a lack of presence, just like fire needs oxygen. So, practice presence like you practice sleep.

Put simply, this means narrowing your focus on what's in front of you now, when you are most anxious. We are wired to create and tell stories (find patterns), but that compulsion brings consequences in the modern world.

Avoid creating stories in your head about where something will go or how it will be received. Focus only on whatever you can do now – in the moment – without reservation.

When something does go bad, trust your first instinct – what you objectively see. For example, when something doesn't go right, listen to the voice that tells you 'that didn't work, now try X' rather than your first *interpretation* of the problem, which will likely tell you 'that screwed up – it's all gone bad.' This approach will allow you to react in the most appropriate way and to do the right thing in the moment. When you trust in your first instinct, without reservation, you've got *presence*. Leave stories to the big screen – there, they're contained.

Go further still by absorbing yourself in something that requires your full presence, like playing a sport. If it's something which absorbs you completely, it will give your head some much needed downtime.

You'll find that presence frees you to make progress on several work areas faster, rather than being anchored unnecessarily on one.

That's the power of presence!

Strategy #31: Beware the Multi-Tasking Myth

To say that you're good at multi-tasking is like pronouncing you're good at playing monkey to whoever says 'dance'.

What you're doing, when you're multi-tasking, is keeping plates spinning – different tasks in series. Multi-tasking is simply rapid task switching, rendering you less productive than doing one thing at a time. Neuroscientists and psychologists have been telling us for decades that the brain can't actually attend to more than one thing at a time. Further, Daniel Levitin, Professor of Behavioral Science at McGill University says that operating this way makes us more tired than if we focused on one thing at a time.

When you multi-task, you're dipping in, dipping out, dipping in, dipping out of tasks and at worst, never getting into anything worthwhile. Each task takes longer than giving it singular focus. You'll realize by now how incredibly inefficient this is. If you multi-task while talking to others, you'll miss subtle non-verbal cues in communication, which is a disaster given that two thirds or more of our face to face communication is through body language.

There's even new research which suggest that incessant multi-tasking lowers IQ by some fifteen points! What's more, studies show that it takes up to 20 minutes for your brain to get back into flow after even a brief interruption.

If that's happening a lot, you're seriously compromised in many ways.

One of the biggest culprits driving multi-tasking in the office is email, which we've already talked about. The advice was to simply disconnect for periods at a time and tackle email in batches at specific times during the day. People also find that deleting their internal instant messenger can be just as profound, enabling them to at least channel all work communication back to one place (email)!

Having said that, there are a couple of instances where multi-tasking can be useful:

- Speed dating. This is a way of getting unpalatable tasks moving (we'll look at speed dating below), but that's really just a deliberate strategy to subvert Gestalt for a benefit. Equally, it's not to be passed off as an efficient way to do anything for long
- PR, in some corporate cultures where busyness is perceived value. It's a practice which will begin to ring hollow as you wonder what your days add up to. Leave it to distractible fad junkies – and task monkeys.

Strategy #32: Rise Early

I used to wonder about the sanity of early risers – those who get up at 4am or 5am to start work.

I've come across a handful of people in my corporate and writing career who do just that, though it eluded me for many years as to why work was so worth getting up so early for. I have on occasion risen early to finish something that needed all the hours that God sent, but those were exceptions.

I've since learnt, through establishing my own writing routine, that early risers aren't in fact psychopaths.

Many impactful people rise early to get important things done before the day moves in to scatter their attention.

By 9am, they've already spent a few hours on what's most important in their work.

That advantage compounds surprisingly quickly.

The early hours are the perfect time for getting into airplane mode. It's a daily slot that's not easily taken away by other demands and distractions. Many experts agree that it's an ideal space for focusing intently on what's important to you. First thing in the morning may also be when your brain's most energized after a night's sleep. Though you will need to get to bed at a reasonable time, this can be made much easier if you simply turn it into a daily habit or routine as we described in part B.

With a routine like that, you'll literally leave the world napping!

Get up early and start on your *one big thing* before the day moves in, and you'll breeze through the rest of it on a psychological high ground.

Questions

1. When are you most likely to drop out of presence? ....

2. What are the main benefits of presence to you and how will you invoke it? ....

3. Do you frequently multi-task and how would you benefit from avoiding it? ....

4. What would you do first each day if you were to rise early?
....

Strategy #33: Manage Your Energy

'Manage Your Energy Not Your Time' by Tony Schwartz and Catherine McCarthy, was published in the *Harvard Business Review* in 2007. I remember feeling change begin inside me the moment I read it and even half laughed to myself at the inevitability of its impact on me as soon as I put it down. I was astonished at the idea and remember that moment as clear as day.

'Manage Your Energy' has since led me on a journey which in the ensuing years, propelled my management and leadership career and even led me to dump things that weren't working in my work. I've since used the principle in coaching others.

Five or so years later, it's an idea that's given me energy and courage to pursue creative interests I would never have considered before. Paradoxically, I was given that article in a role I no longer endure.

People say that money is your most important asset. Others say it's time. But my view is that it's energy. With energy everything that's possible becomes plausible; without it, all the time or money in the world won't help you achieve the impact you want.

You may have noticed that energy management is a philosophy that permeates a lot of the strategies in this series.

Think of your brain as a gas tank that fills overnight and empties during the day. Imagine that gas is glucose and understand that *everything* draws a little or a lot from your mental energy bank.

When you listen to noise, your brain works a little harder to concentrate. When you make a choice to exercise or not, that small decision can use a lot of energy dealing with conflict or touting willpower. Solving significant problems at work depletes a huge amount of that gas tank.

Each time we shift our attention from one thing to the next – social media posts, email to email or conversation to conversation, our brains use a little energy to make each mental transition. When you do this hundreds of times a day, the resultant fatigue diminishes your ability to regulate emotions, remain patient with people or challenges around you and even compromises your ability to focus. This precipitates a downward spiral of energy and motivation, leaving us spent by the end of the day. That's when the frontal cortex winds down and the amygdala takes control. When you're pre-disposed to negativity, you can imagine how disheartening that can leave you feeling. All of that results from simply mismanaging your energy levels!

It goes without saying, then, that you should protect your mental energy like your wallet.

Fresh food and lots of water obviously provide the glucose for muscle and brain function, but energy management isn't just about re-fueling the furnace.

So, what releases tied up energy?

- Clarity, whether due to alignment of people like a magnet to north, a compelling vision of something bigger than oneself, the completion of an endeavor, recognition, and good relationships
- Inspiration from outside or from within
- Physical movement unshackles the mind when it's stuck. Humans are built to walk and run and oxygen that pumps your veins ignites the glucose in your brain.

And what devours energy unnecessarily?

- Uncertainty and ambiguity[15] whether due to conflict, fear, anger, frustration, disappointment, anxiety, distraction, and so on and so on
- Physical and mental fatigue, which are self-reinforcing downward spirals. They have the potential to kill otherwise positive relationships. Fatigue kills mood and a low mood compromises the choices you make, says a study from Stanford University. The study shows that those in a good mood more readily tackle challenging tasks,

---

[15] Humans find ambiguity stressful. If we can predict outcomes and reduce uncertainty, even the occasional surprise is easier to accept. But if the outcomes remain unpredictable — if no amount of adapting to overcome ambiguity helps — people get stressed quickly, and that devours energy.

whereas a low mood often leads to pleasure seeking (buying stuff, goofing off) as a way to feel better. Good mood, it seems, can be used as a resource for getting important things done.

Think about one of the most satisfying moments you've had at work. It was probably a moment when you knew exactly what you were doing, how to do it and by when you had to complete. You probably completed the activity without distraction. You may have worked with colleagues on the same wavelength and you probably had all the tools and information you needed to hand. You achieved an outcome and it was valued by whoever received it.

It all felt like pushing a snowball downhill, did it not? There's clarity, energy and movement in that example.

Now picture the opposite. You're on a project with ambiguity. People are pulling in different directions and have different priorities. You're not sure whether the work you're doing is the best thing, or even the right thing. You want to keep moving, but there's a multitude of options and you're not sure which is best. You expend energy trying to get clarity from managers and align people, but you don't really get the support you need. You decide to plough ahead anyway for the sake of progress, but find that you eventually have to backtrack or change course. It's late in the afternoon and you're normally tired at this time – unsurprisingly things feel bleak. You're working flat out but you're not sure what you've achieved or exactly where you're going.

All of that is the signature of uncertainty, lack of clarity and simply running out of steam.

Sadly, the latter is a common picture in modern offices, whereas the former could be micro-moments in your daily work. However, there's a clear message here for leaders and team members alike:

To maximize energy, you have to work to find clarity and tackle uncertainty head on. One of the best ways is to break down uncertainty into smaller – more certain – chunks.

It can also be helpful to construct your own energy chart throughout the day to become aware of repeated patterns.

When you *feel* down, try to understand what, from the items above, may have driven that. It's usually one of fatigue, hunger or thirst and those alone will almost always lead to disagreeableness and illusions of disappointment.

They alone can fuel resentment and conflict unnecessarily.

As you do this daily, you'll find that you can learn to pre-empt these low moments by eating effectively, but also withdrawing and resting where you may normally have simply tried to push harder for diminishing returns.

A Typical Daily Energy Curve

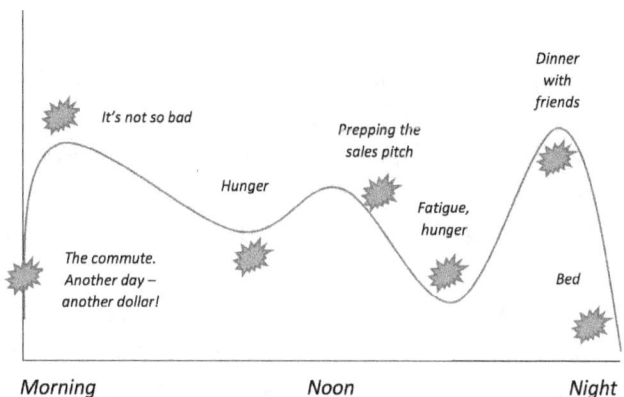

Learn to recognize when you have low energy and try the following:

- Eat first. Dried fruit, nuts and seed are good. Avoid caffeine and highly processed or sugary foods. You're looking for *small* quantities of high-G foods which give slow release of energy over an extended period. Don't overfill, or simply digesting what you ate will devour any energy you wanted
- Practice perception management. Avoid cogitating – especially on the purpose of life or it's challenges. Without fail, things *feel* worse when energy is low, because your perception is the first thing that crashes
- If you must think, think upsides. A ratio of five *upsides* to one *downside* is balanced!

- Avoid tackling something difficult, simply by trying harder. You'll quickly get to diminishing returns from your effort
- Engross yourself in something calming which you really enjoy or something do socially beneficial. Do these on autopilot without having to justify their value. They will give you a mental boost precisely when you most need it
- Walk and get fresh air. This helps to disconnect your brain
- Withdraw and rest – even if reluctantly. You simply can't avoid your physical need for rest and you can't fight low physical and mental energy by simply trying harder. Look at some of the energy-boosting techniques below, when we talk about disconnection.

To boost energy and ready yourself for performance, try visualization.

This is simply story-construction and appeals to the subconscious to trigger habitual behavior as well as override limiting beliefs. Call it mental preparation, or even muscle memory. It can lead to self-belief which is important when faced with obstacles.

Having said that, I'd advise you not to get lost in romantic notions of blissful self-belief. Your subconscious is open to delusion and mental movies aren't the same thing as reality. Pleasurable visualization releases serotonin, which reduces our alertness to the (perhaps harsh) realities around us. There are *always* factors off-stage that you can't, or don't see, and over which you have no control. Most of all, there's something called the competence cycle in your way, which we discuss later. You don't want to be the bewildered X-factor-type dropout when reality finally hits home in the glare of the public!

Your confidence is much better served instead by genuine skill, a track record, strong options – and presence.

Those things are indisputable, whether or not they hit home when it really counts.

Questions

1. Draw your own energy curve. What does it look like? ....
2. What will you do when your energy's low? ....

Strategy #34: Speed Date and Try Not to Finish

Having plugged the need for clarity, I'll now ask you to get comfortable with things incomplete, unresolved and unfinished.

Sometimes, you simply won't be able to conjure up energy at will. Doing things, even important things, can often feel like pushing snowballs uphill. Sometimes that's down to a lack of clarity and sometimes fatigue. There's inertia lurking inside the unfamiliar. But a lot of the time, the reason can be a complete mystery.

A good technique for low-energy situations is speed dating.

Yes, you just go off on a round of speed dating to clear out the cobwebs. Here's how:

- **Make a small start** to honor your commitment and get your brain engaged. You just want to give procrastination the heave ho
- **Line up a few intransigent items** on the basis they are important or necessary and decide **to spend no more than 5 minutes on each. That could be just 5 minutes of simply getting** your pens or paintbrushes out – and no more. Remember this *isn't* about finishing – it *is* about starting. Even *you*

can spare just 5 minutes out of 24 hours on anything
- **Stop the clock at 5 minutes** no matter how far you get, and be sure to leave each item mid-flow if you can
- **Move on** to the next task and repeat
- **Repeat** that whole process later in the day or week, adding another 5 minutes to each round, so you're now focused 10 minutes on each task before moving to the next one. Remember to stop dead at 10 minutes. What you'll notice is that your brain will want to get back to the unfinished tasks, rather than procrastinate as before. Congratulations, you've overcome inertia and got the ball rolling
- **Run with a task** once it takes on a life of its own. What you'll find, miraculously, is that you're now pushing that same snowball downhill, almost effortlessly.

All it takes is: first finding the right moment; then releasing energy. What a difference!

What you're doing here is leveraging Gestalt in you favor. Remember that the brain dislikes leaving things incomplete or unresolved, feeling compelled to seek completion. You're simply getting your brain's attention by connecting to it in a way that it was designed.

A big payoff of this technique, other than getting important things done, is that you've conserved your mental energy by avoiding a battle with willpower.

Question

1. Which unpalatable but necessary tasks are you ready to speed date?..

Strategy #35: Persist and Build Competence

Persistence, also known as grit, is key in tackling anything challenging at work – and everything can feel challenging if we're in a company that constantly grows and moves into new territory.

Understanding the limitation of, and shedding the lure of working solely within our preference box is now more frequently the norm for many of us.

So how do you enhance persistence within yourself or your team safely? Just push harder? Do night shifts as well as the day? Motivate yourself and others with vision statements?

I find vision to be a weak muscle and here's why: it's up against something called the competence cycle.

The truth is that no amount of great advice or trumpeting talk will move you through the cycle to a point where you can have any impact at all. Instead, you'll need to do the work.

Furthermore, vision is most likely to rear its head precisely when you're at your most gullible. That's stage 1, or Unconscious Incompetence.

Instead, if you spend your time doing something you love and utilize the techniques of habit and routine you've already read about, you will get a long way quickly. Motivation might prop you up, but you still need to walk the long way round! It's vital to persist through the cycle and face and overcome obstacles with humility – and good feedback.

So, what if you or your team are facing something new and scary?

First, understand the stages of venturing into new territory and where precisely you'll lose your confidence. Prepare for the worst before things get better.

Stages of Competence (Overlaid with Gladwell's Mastery Clock Time[16], Pareto and Kübler-Ross[17])

	Layperson	Authority
	Stage 2 **Conscious** **Incompetence** Gladwell: 0-8k hours Pareto ~80% Kübler-Ross: Anger, Bargaining, Depression	**Stage 3** **Unconscious** **Competence** Gladwell: 8k-10k hours Pareto: ~20% Kübler-Ross: Acceptance
	Stage 1 **Unconscious** **Incompetence** Gladwell: 0 hours Pre Kübler-Ross: Euphoria, Denial	**Stage 4** **Conscious** **Competence** Gladwell: 10k+ hours

Stage 1: Unconscious Incompetence

Stage 1 is usually a departure point from vision, determination and ambition, all of which put us on the front foot to venture boldly into new territory with unbridled enthusiasm. Like natural tranquilizers, they shield our eyes from the inevitable challenges to come, giving our optimism biases free reign.

---

[16] Malcolm Gladwell postulates, in Outliers, that it takes 10,000 hours of practice to master a skill
[17] Elisabeth Kübler-Ross modeled the stages of grief to acceptance in her 1969 book, On Death and Dying

It is great to be on the front foot, because without it, humanity would never do anything.

But how many times have you said to yourself with hindsight, *If I knew what it would take, I would never have started.* What this points to is the feeling of early-stage incompetence and that's inevitable when you tackle anything new.

The natural tranquilizers flooding our brains keep us away from what we don't know. Call these bogeys: the unknown unknowns, they're masked by overconfidence.

This is also the stage during which the vast majority of undiscovered *talent*, particularly young talent, lays neglected. It's the stage in which sparks fly – or don't.

What will help you persist here is to recognize, early on, that you may be walking around in cloud cuckoo land with any new endeavor.

However unpalatable it may seem, it's best to move into stage 2 as quickly as possible, by casting your spotlight on potential points of failure and weaknesses in your capabilities.

Talk to others and see where they went wrong, then expect to have some learning to do. You're a novice in a new game and you aren't yet aware of the conventions and ground rules established over a long period before you. Nevertheless, you move in gleefully, expecting to singlehandedly change the game. The veterans grin quietly at the bloody nose about to come your way.

Do your training, and learn to distrust your own stage 1 hype. You're trying to put your incompetency on the table so you can tackle it systematically.

It also pays to remember at this stage that 'work' often equals 're-work'. This is a quality mantra. Your first idea, draft, or impression is *never* good. It takes re-work and creative process to get your work to good. As an example, the Boeing aircraft company is said to require *seven* iterations of components to achieve a desired *minimum* level of quality. If you're writing a book, for instance, that would mean seven drafts! If you're learning an instrument, that means endless repetition.

If you find this hard to swallow, you're probably in denial. This is the onset of Stage 2. Well, at least you're moving in the right direction!

Stage 2: Conscious Incompetence

Well, done – you now realize you have a lot to learn *and* that your own eyes could never have given you a full picture of what lay ahead. Now you can embrace learning, obtain the resource you need and give yourself half a chance of reaching your goal.

But, everything begins to feel harder than first expected, because if you persist, you're working

outside of your preference box. You're in early-stage learning, which is precisely when most people head back to the safety of their preferences. It's a frustrating time because there's a gap between your expectations of what's possible and what you're actually able to achieve. The pros make it look easy, but you simply can't. You need to keep working. It's frustrating.

Professor Angela Duckworth a psychologist at the University of Pennsylvania has shown that *grit* (or resilience) is more important than talent or intelligence in predicting successful outcomes. You can help yourself enormously in stage 2, by being passionately interested in what you're doing and by having a sense of purpose (we explored why this is an important resource in Volume 1). You'll also benefit from forming a habit of working on your challenges frequently and systematically. Then, using techniques, discussed under the power of positivity above, renew your hope whenever you face setbacks. With an arsenal like that, you'll have half a chance of making it out of stage 2 with only a handful of bullet holes.

You'll be learning voraciously, but learning uses a lot of energy. Expect it to be mentally taxing.

You may be irritable or angry and berate yourself for not having what it takes – because you don't just yet. You'll try to negotiate an easy way through, convincing yourself that half-baked outputs are sufficient. But the world reminds you otherwise. You'll feel like throwing in the towel – most people do.

If you can calm your nerves here and stay the course in stage 2, you'll leave the majority hitting their snooze button.

Now consider that persistence requires energy and hours. You can't do that with something you hate. At best you'll be watching the clock, then clocking out early.

That's why, by stage 2, it pays enormously to chase something you genuinely love to do if you're after big impact. Finding your passion and motivation was one of the essentials in Volume 1.

Using the 80:20 Pareto principle (see, it applies to everything), you may spend up to 80% of your 10,000 hours to mastery before the end of Stage 2, and it probably won't be the fun you initially imagined with all that vision and self-talk at the beginning.

However, if you do love every minute of what you're doing, you're generally unassailable from here on in.

Stage 3: Unconscious Competence

This is where you get to act like characters on the silver screen. You now have that special something that you never saw creeping up during all the stage 2 hours. But others now see it from afar.

They see the potential, which ***they*** taught you to downplay in stage 2, having called for humility. Your overconfidence and brazenness, last seen in stage 1, is long gone.

Stage 3 is the beginning of stories. Sadly, this isn't a reality for 80% of people, who ditched their dreams during stage 2 (or were booed off-stage, never to return). You're now amongst the 20% who managed to stay the course and get this far.

You've genuinely learnt something and it begins to show. Things start to feel a little easier and even rewarding.

You make it look easy and people, new to you, mistake your stage 2 graft for a *gift*. At this stage, you have well-honed skills. You, however, either loved every minute of the graft or have blocked it out. You've stopped fighting delusion and can't see what the fuss is about. You accept things the way they are. Your head's moved on and the trenches are a distant memory.

Using Pareto again, expect to spend 20% of your 10,000 hours towards mastery here. You're now known as *Good* and heading towards *Great*, in the words of Jim Collins.

Stage 4: Conscious Competence

You own the stage during the final phase.

You're one of the Greats in the top 3-5% of your game. Your skills have transformed into what looks like art. Your subconscious conjures connections that you yourself couldn't rationally create. You know which way's up, because you said it should be so. You've now built an unbeatable track record and you know it too. You're at the top of *your* tree.

It's taken years, but it can go in one of two ways from here.

What normally derails impactful people in stage 4 is a failure to recognize the need for sustainability. Things change and dominance gets challenged. Even boredom moves in to knock you off your perch.

If you like what you do, you'll need a few defenses to protect your territory and maintain your advantage. You'll also benefit from extending your footprint into other areas by applying transferable skills in creative ways. We'll look at strategies for creativity below and you can read about competition in Volume 4.

The biggest problem the rest of us mortals face is that we normally only see the stage 4 people being trumpeted, or trumpeting themselves as examples of good.

This trumpeting is a mainstay of PR, leadership spiel, stories and media. Stage 4 PR underpins *'it could be you'* stories. We consume these stories during stage 1, when we're most gullible.

But you must, by now, realize that stage 4 is a very small tip of a very large iceberg. We rarely, if ever, see the voluminous stage 1s or 2s – under the waterline – being lauded, having fallen by the wayside.

Stage 1 and 2 are Unconscious Incompetence and the Ladder of Interference all in one shot. These stages are largely what give rise to the planning fallacy – failing to account for what exists off stage.[18]

We're generally miserable at estimating the time it takes to develop new capabilities. The brain learns and adapts, to physical skills in particular, at a painfully slow pace.

There is an upside, however. Most things do get easier with practice and persistence.

You also quickly find yourself in rarified company when you stick with something challenging and outside of your preference.

But the only way to sustain that type of impact easily is through self-awareness. In particular, that means understanding and taming the positive and negative biases which are coded right into your DNA. You can read more about them in Volume 1.

---

[18] You can read about The ladder of Inference in Volume 1 of the series

Questions

1. When have you begun a *new* endeavor which didn't succeed as expected? ....

2. Did the competency cycle play a role e.g. unrealistic expectations in stage 1, lack of skills in stage 2, lack of persistence in stage 3? ....

3. Did you succeed at an endeavor, only to see your success dissipate? ....

4. Did competition or boredom in stage 4 play a role? ....

Strategy #36: Schedule Rest and Play before Work

We work so hard to earn a living, that we often forget *the living*.

And working hard takes resilience – a key success factor in the most demanding of workplaces. It's the ability to persevere effectively through a continuous stream of challenges and obstacles over a prolonged period. Research suggests, nevertheless, that resilience varies substantially amongst us. So how can we help ourselves to remain in good shape? Remember first: until *your* basic needs are met, you can't fully meet the needs of *others*. Second: being sufficiently well rested underpins resilience.

As you begin to pay attention to the idea of energy management, it will become obvious that being tired every day is like shooting yourself in the foot. It only takes a tiny drop in energy to castrate your ability to make good choices: how you spend your time, what you eat, whether you exercise or not. Your ability to persist with challenging mental tasks goes out of the window. That includes getting work done, making difficult calls, and so on.

Procrastination will be your constant companion when you're tired.

Conversely, you will feel like an outperformer, full of gusto and energy, if everyone else around you is sleepwalking while you're fully engaged.

When you get tired, it's natural for your mind to slip into time-based thinking. That's a lack of presence.

Woah, what does that mean? That means projecting into the future or thinking about the past. Things like: *I wish that didn't happen*, or *that will turn out badly*, or *that's gonna be a problem*, or *I wish I was like X*. These thoughts are the antithesis of presence.

Since you can't physically deal with those thoughts now, your limbs are essentially paralyzed, yet your mind wants to act. This sets up an anxiety gap in your head, because things don't feel quite right. Your subconscious gets the instinct for flight or fight, but it can't tell the difference between fantasy and reality (watch an action-packed movie – it's not real, nevertheless you feel it). It doesn't know reason, because that's not it's job – it's role is to govern emotion and instinct.

This is a self-reinforcing cycle because time-based thinking becomes prevalent when you're tired. The emotional center takes charge when you can't think straight. Shadows loom large to the emotional center and that's great on the screen, but horribly paralyzing in the real world of work. The trouble is that you can't deal with either the past or the future in the here and now.

You stop connecting to others, because you don't have the energy to hear and engage in mental challenges.

So, when you're tired:

Procrastination moves in. Challenging mental tasks are more likely to be parked until the next day. This includes the avoidance of listening and learning, which take significant cognitive effort. Procrastination and avoidance are always an easier path.

Decisions are compromised. You're more likely to take shortcuts and make poor decisions and choices when you're tired. After all, is it ever a good choice to put off something important until tomorrow? Studies have shown that lack of sleep affects the brain's executive center first, resulting in reduced frontal cortex activity. Evaluation, self-control and rational decision-making suffer as a result, while the more primitive amygdala keeps working. That means you rely more on emotion, intuition and impulsivity than objectivity, and that's disastrous for decision-making, because intuition is highly fallible. It's like drink driving – you *always* believe you're okay, though that's *never* actually the case.

Weight becomes a problem. What about decisions regarding what you eat? You make rash, easy choices by picking up unhealthy food in supermarkets. Why? In a word – easy. Easy to prepare ready meals for instance. The result: weight gain. Studies have shown that 'satiety hormones' drop when you're tired. You're less satisfied with what you've eaten, so you eat more.

You're distracted and focus on minutiae. If I was putting off something challenging whenever tired in the morning, what was I doing instead? Well, because I was tired, I was probably picking off the easy stuff like admin, paying bills, clearing my inbox and so on. In all likelihood, I was also deferring the important more difficult stuff, like writing a report, or going to the gym or just *doing* the work.

Your tolerance takes a battering. You can of course function *okay* without adequate sleep year after year – you won't just drop dead. But once that becomes your norm, you're compromised without really being aware of it, because you forget what *good* was like.

You become desensitized to the things going on around you. If you're less empathetic, or your patience for those around you plummets, you cannot be effective while collaborating with others in the office. You'll miss subtle non-verbal cues in communication simply because your brain doesn't have the energy to process them. Those who are sleep deprived have a harder time processing facial expressions, shows a 2014 study in the Experimental Brain Research. Another recent study from Tel Aviv university also showed that your ability to separate the important, from the merely urgent, plummets too.

As you can see, there's a cascade of problems that starts to add up easily and almost without any real awareness. If you come to work regularly tired, you're compromised – I don't care what your culture says. Your reaction to sleep deprivation was wired into your

DNA long before someone conjured up your corporate culture. If you operate like this consistently, you compromise not only your own work, but also that of your colleagues and your organization.

So, what's actually happening when you can't get enough shut eye, for instance? The mind has trouble moving from what's known as the alpha state, to the theta state of sleep. The frontal cortex, still engaged, continues to scan and rationalize patterns and problems (however menial), looking for imagined danger. This is a rational process, which may be great during the day, but one which is debilitating and needs turning off at bedtime. Research shows that those between the ages of twenty and thirty-four are the most vulnerable from effects of sleep loss according to a study by Ashridge Executive Education in the UK.

Here are some strategies to rejuvenate during down-times. Some will help you to commandeer the zzzzs and calm incessant self-talk (which prevents the brain switching off for rest):

- Discombobulate your head. If you're observant, you may have noticed there's a sudden loss of coherence in your train of thought at the precise point of sleep, and so much so, that it becomes impossible to recall what you were thinking just moments before. Try to replicate and induce this state by picturing *random, disconnected* objects which have no relation to one other for 5-10 minutes. It could be any random steam of anything. This randomness interrupts the

frontal cortex problem solving apparatus, which is the part of the brain which keeps you alert. You can also do this in any part of the day, scanning random objects around you for mental downtime.
- Breath in for 4 seconds through your nose, hold your breath for 7 seconds, then breath out for 8 seconds. Try this several times at five- or ten-minute intervals. This procedure acts like a natural tranquilizer
- Put your thoughts inside an imaginary box, with the option to take them out if necessary
- Focus intently on an imaginary ball darting around an imaginary pinball machine for ten minutes
- See your thoughts being carried away by thought bubbles
- Create a simple mental movie of a boring, repetitive bedtime routine. Play the movie in your head daily at bedtimes until the experience becomes the habit
- Remove electronics from your bedroom and go to bed five minutes earlier each fortnight, until you are getting enough rest. This disassociates your bed with habitual rational, frontal cortex thinking.
- Get daylight into your eyeballs between 0630 and 0830 to set your circadian rhythm for sleep the subsequent night.
- Schedule downtime or playtime *before* you schedule worktime. What do you like to play? What are you looking forward to? Is it in your diary regularly? Allow your mind to wander during your breaks.

Questions

1. Does tiredness impact your work? ....
2. How can you recognize tiredness e.g. energy curve? ....
3. What strategy above will you adopt to avoid tiredness? ..

Summary D

We've just completed the fourth part of our productivity circle – focus.

We learnt about the importance of finding it to do our work and using apps to help us tune out the world when required. We looked at presence to maintain our focus and avoid multi-tasking our important activities. We read about rising early to make big gains at the start of each day, the importance of managing energy and speed dating to unstick unpalatable tasks. You cycled round the competence curve so you now know what to expect as you progress through new challenges. Finally, we examined the importance of rest and play.

All of this will help you remain focused – and if you focus well, you'll significantly outpace others in creating impactful work.

E. Diversity and Distraction

This will now sound like a contradiction, having talked about focus and avoidance of distractions.

What I'm asking you to do here is open up to the world and allow distraction in. Go find it. Enjoy yourself a little!

This is especially important if you've become a focus ninja using earlier techniques in this book. Diversity is vital, so you receive input from informal channels and avoid getting locked into your own narrow point of view. It's also the seed of creativity as we'll read below.

The point here is two-fold: to avoid boredom in your routines and habits and to cultivate diversity as one of the fundamental components of creativity.

Because we're experience-seeking creatures, we get bored when things work like clockwork and routine. We're made to be distracted by rustling bushes and in order to keep that fundamental capability alive and well oiled, our brains keep looking out for distraction.

Boredom stifles energy, persistence, creativity, empathy and focus. Distraction brings story, experience and energy into our lives.

A degree of distraction is especially important if you're in a tight routine or rigid habit at work. Sooner or later your subconscious will want to escape the shackles and will do so just when you *don't* need it.

If you don't allow for at least some goofing, it will come looking for you. Be opportunistic. Allow happy accidents to happen.

One of the biggest challenges at work today is spending all our time in distracted mode, with a storm of communication coming at us. When we get into this mode, we have to make sure we don't stay there too long!

Strategy #37: Get Creative and Challenge the Status Quo

Creativity, in a nutshell, is fundamentally about combining diverse ideas in new ways. The late Steve Jobs commented that it's "just connecting things."

It's about exploiting and integrating disparate ideas in ways, perhaps never done before. It's not copying, nor stealing, but simply making better use of what's already there. Sir Isaac Newton summed this up perfectly when he said of his mathematical discoveries, 'I was simply standing on the shoulder of giants.'

It's said that everything that needs inventing has already been invented, but whether or not that's true – of the bit-parts at least – it's certainly not true of all the possible combinations of those bit-parts.

In this day and age, with fast-moving global markets, multitudes of new producers in every market and new channels, mastery of a particular domains may be headed for obsolescence.

The future – and the present – already belongs to creatives.

Mastery may still count in a closed circuit or a deeply physical skill – perhaps like Formula 1 or professional tennis. Hand-eye co-ordination still takes years of painstaking repetition to develop.

For at least a decade or two, however, more and more industries and professions have had to relinquish gate-keeping strategies to protect their dominance and the status quo. Publishing is the current victim. The cost of creating and distributing new media has dropped precipitously and access has become abundant. If you're inventing iPads, publishing music, or writing software, creativity is king.

Furthermore, commerciality determines whether or not something's worth mastering at all.

Old domains are increasingly disrupted. For instance, it may make less sense to master an orchestral instrument when fewer people go to live concerts. More people now make music on computers and post it online. In turn, that trend has already disrupted myriad industries built around concert going. It's commercial viability that influences what's possible or not.

It's necessary, then, to pay attention to new technology, because that's what fundamentally drives new ways to create, channel and market *existing* ideas.

Talking, for instance, wasn't new when cell phones arrived, but the devices allowed us to talk in *new places*. Books weren't invented by Amazon – the retailer simply allowed more people to have *easier access* for less (including authors). Both of these technologies met *existing* wants in *new* ways.

Here are a few examples of other combinations at work:

- Auctions combined with digital distribution gave rise to eBay
- Large displays combined with small smartphones gave rise to iPads
- Re-skinned, old operating systems, with a new bell or whistle (as well as a new number) gave rise to 'new' operating systems e.g. Windows X.

Creativity – Example: Operating in a Pre-Existing Market for Portable Music

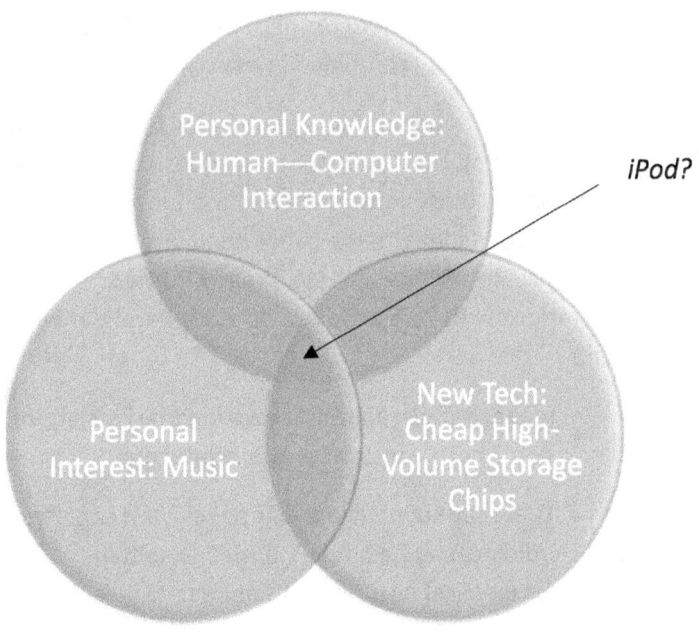

This is a good example of initiative and invention, born of combination and evolution – not revolution.

Corporates pay people to simply dream up new combinations of existing ideas, which are aimed at established markets. New technology permits intellectual property, personal interest and knowledge to sprout new products and services. They often arrive unannounced, simply adding features one small step at a time over a sustained period of evolution. Over time and with deep enough pockets, they often come to dominate their markets.

What you need, then, is a diversity of experience and interest.

Many creatives over history, though probably known for just one major contribution, had diverse interests which they combined in new ways.

It pays to understand commercial limitations on creativity. Revolution, unfortunately, doesn't come with a paycheck, so most consumers and producers aren't out for it. Good ideas, in the other hand, are communicable and fit 80% into already formed expectations with 20% added on (there's Pareto at work again).

Ideas that are aimed at existing markets are of lower risk for both consumers and producers.

That may sound like a dampener on creativity, but it should instead be a relief. It means neither waiting for mystical inspiration to appear, nor having to boil the ocean to create something *new*. Consign revolution to dreams, the big screen and fiction.

At the same time, budgetary constraints stifle creativity. Is necessity is the mother of invention? Not entirely, in my view. The phrase only holds to a certain degree.

Necessity, instead, is the mother of survival – not breakthrough.

Why? Brains are lazy and take time off at the first opportunity once survival is assured. Genuine creativity, however, requires freedom from artificial constraints like time and money, because most creative ideas seem to emerge randomly. When your team's working to tight deadlines, you can be certain they're mostly filling out templates. By implication, working to tight deadlines and budgets generates mediocre output.

It's rumored that Apple's Steve Jobs removed budgetary constraints from employees and simply asked them to produce their *best work*. The impact of the iPhone speaks for itself. Imagine for a moment if George Lucas stopped writing *Star Wars* after his first draft because of budget constraints. Well, he wrote at least four drafts – to no tight deadlines, all over several years. The results, again, speak for themselves.

Creativity is also almost always an accident of time, but can be precipitated by good process.

When you have an illuminating resolution to a problem, you're often left wondering why neither you nor anyone else had ever thought of it before. In the moment, it seems so obvious. Often, the only ingredients which brought it to the fore were time, and working the problem.

The answer appeared like a happy accident – and this is key.

You often don't have the answer first, then proceed to flesh it out. Instead, you work the problem until a solution *emerges*. Creativity is simply a well-honed process, not a heaven-sent muse.

So, what does a creative process look like?

Creative Process

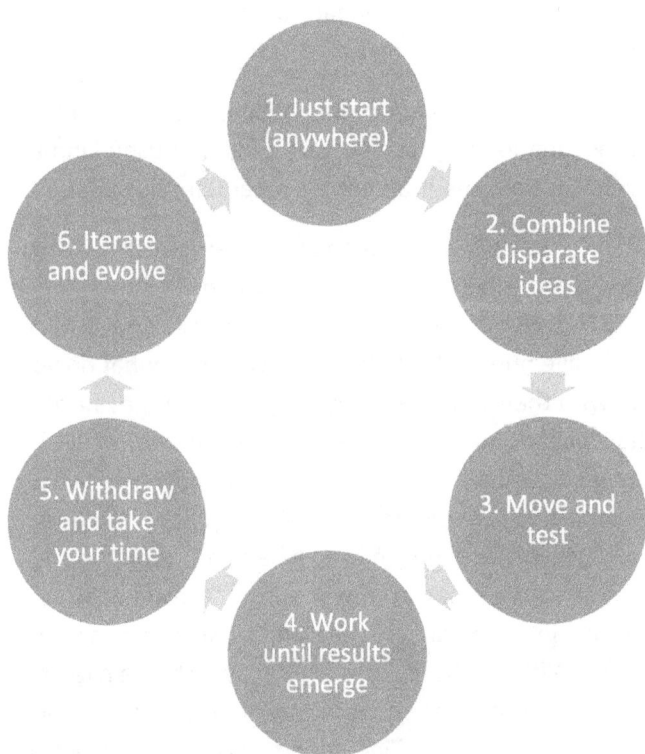

1. Just start (anywhere)

Take any impression, whatever it is, without knowing all the answers or the finished output. You can also start with a known challenge or a problem which frustrates you and is screaming for a solution.

Your aim is to be "passionately curious, rather than intelligent" at this stage – as Albert Einstein once said of himself. It helps enormously to have a strong motivator, as we explored in Volume 1, to provide the seed of persistence in the face of inevitable setbacks which may come your way.

Once you begin with an idea, allow some time for incubation as you seek out and gather useful input which defines the problem (or potential solution).

Some form of structure or framework for your ideas can help enormously here. You picked these up as you moved through the competence cycle above. When you have hundreds of ideas flying around, what do you do with them? Where do you put them so they have half a chance to come together as a coherent whole? How will you test that you're at least observing well established conventions, if any? Consider for instance writing a book: simply having a beginning, middle and end structure – or the conventions of the genre you're writing in – provide structure and frameworks for your ideas. Without these, your work may just be a pile of related but incoherent ideas. Say, you're setting up a business: having a business model allows you to put the right activities and ideas in the right order, so they don't fall through the cracks or distract you at the wrong time. Frameworks reveal priorities and help you to focus on what's important in the moment.

Structure and frameworks are also used as tools to communicate your ideas clearly in stage 2. In that context, they suggest expertise and experience, well rounded ideas and logical thinking.

This is also a good stage in which to set aside at least some regular time to mentally do little or nothing. Even better, try to do this when you're tired! Surprisingly, this provides a good mental state for creative ideas, because it's a time when your frontal cortex is naturally more relaxed and less goal focused. The rational problem solving apparatus is less active allowing the subconscious to create unforeseen neural connections in the background. Further, you can help yourself by avoiding stimulants like caffeine, which we all know, fire up the executive center of the brain. It's in these moments that exciting ideas get a chance to bubble up to the surface, without the constraints of rational challenge. Creative and analytical thinking are somewhat mutually exclusive.

So, when do you do all this? Well, it's unlikely to be at work of all places! What we tend to do in the office is slurp coffee, think analytically, kill embryonic ideas which undermine our personal agendas and present logical arguments that are as free from personal risk as possible! For all its touting, you can see that corporate life is generally not set up to be innovative nor creative. Analytics are important, but you really want to leave that for the subsequent stage below.

Nevertheless, we need to be at least somewhat 'creative' at work, so what do you do, especially with groups? Well, groups, especially, epitomize all the problems described above, so it's best, at first, to have individuals work alone on problems. This prevents what's known as groupthink and compromise when groups simply listen to the 'loudest voice' in the room. (Review Operating Modes in Volume 1 to learn more about the impact of personalities in the office).

And what if you have trouble generating ideas? Experts suggest that you put in some constraints or boundaries within which to work. This could mean observation of well-established conventions and beginning with lowered expectations, simply to allow people get started easily.

2. **Combine your ideas with other disparate ideas with a good fit**

This is otherwise known as divergent thinking – *collecting* ideas from a diverse range of sources or people who perhaps began by working alone. It's helpful to cultivate a sense of exploration and adventure.

This is where you get illuminating moments – the Eurekas.

This is where you find your *Trojan Horse* – Odysseus, having tried all avenues to overcome the Trojans directly, re-framed the problem of 'defeating them', to 'how to deceive them' instead (as a result, he sent in his infamous Trojan Horse, deceiving them from the inside, after failing to forcefully defeat them from the outside).

But remember that, while you may have big ideas, most others around you probably don't. Break your big ideas down and bring them back towards the center of the bell curve if you expect to take other people with you.

Remember that creativity has to come in a package that the Averages can cope with – for instance books have structure and convention so people can understand them. Don't expect the Averages to operate far beyond the middle of the curve, or take a leap of faith.

But there's a paradox, which you can either digest, or can't.

If you want to create something spectacular, expect others to be confused at first. Expect that they may not to be able to journey with you. In fact, the more you experience resistance, the more likely it is that you have the trait of something genuinely new, that others will understand, only when completed.

3. **Move and test**

To be creative, you have to expose yourself to at least some risk. Promoters and entrepreneurs, especially (the naturally creative types), will benefit from trialing their ideas in different locations and different times, with different people, to see if they work in all weathers. It's important to first draft or blueprint ideas to see whether they are more substantive than the first impressions which gave rise to them. Is there enough meat on the bone for something coherent, complete and cohesive to emerge at the end?

You must have the courage to get your work into the world, to see if it works even though it may not be complete at this stage. Manage expectations and try not to be defensive. You need to avoid getting too attached to your ideas, but simply present them instead. You can do this by mentally stepping out of your own head and *pretending* to advice a friend. Thinking in the third person temporarily disengages the amygdala (and all its emotional baggage), allowing the reasoning frontal cortex to weigh in with analytics and rational thought.

And this is the perfect time to get analytical, because your initial impressions are often deluding and can be no more than fleeting observations, lacking real substance. Initial impressions feel good but often don't add up to anything viable on their own, contrary to popular beliefs regarding fabled moments of genius.

You don't want to spend years enamored with an idea that never had legs in the first place – if only you'd slowed down enough to check.

Get verification.

It's also the perfect time for convergent thinking – connecting the dots in new ways with people working together again. Seek diverse experience and take your time. You don't want to rush and suffer lapses in reasoning.

But don't be too harsh. You want to recognize underdeveloped ideas for what they are and not expect fully formed solutions.

Nevertheless, while you're busy embracing diversity, try to go with something within the realm of acceptability. By this, I mean, whatever respects convention or has a very good reason to innovate it.

4. Work your ideas, until results emerge

Creativity emerges from the work itself, not necessarily from impressions up front. The brain throws out new ideas randomly, but most often, only after you've identified and begun to work a problem. You can't sit back and expect your big idea to drop into your lap fully formed or even functional at the outset. It never does.

It can be helpful to sprint through the initial creation, creating as much substance as possible without excessive editing. Your aim is to give shape and coherence to your idea, not to perfect the first iteration. This is where you discover the unknowns and questions that arise from whatever it is you are doing. You can do a sprint during stage 1 above too.

It's helpful to invite further convergent thinking at this point. Get people together again to iterate or combine different features or solutions to a problem you're trying to solve.

5. Withdraw and take your time

Walk[19]. Go play. Sleep on it if you must. Your subconscious remains at work on creative challenges in the background when you withdraw for a time. It is *the* source of all your creative ideas.

When you reduce the pressure of delivery, you also tend to avoid the obvious first solution, which may not be that creative at all. You're allowing room for the sub-conscious to incubate the problem further and creating the space for different parts of your brain to pitch in to the challenge. Connection forming between neurones isn't a conscious process so you can't hear or feel the cogs turning, but trust that it's happening and wait for the Eureka moments! In his book *On Writing*, Stephen King talks about allowing the first draft of a novel to *rest*. "Let it rest." Let your first draft rest.

A new study from Stanford University has shown that people are more creative when walking instead of sitting i.e. not what do we do in every office, everywhere, all day and every day! You're trying to do something pleasurable to release serotonin, a feel good neuro-chemical which unleashes creativity.

Suspend reality to achieve creativity. Run a marathon, climb a mountain, learnt to compose, take a career break... hell, chose poverty for a while. When you're suspended somewhere in the ethereal, there are

---

[19] Walking unleashes creativity. It's as if changing stimuli, light physical effort and extra oxygen untether the imagination from habitual ways of thinking. Habits stifle creativity.

no earthly structures or social conventions to trigger habitual ways of thinking. New things have to emerge when you put yourself in that zone regularly. It's known that you're more creative when you're tired for instance, because the brain is less coherent and rational.

This is where you manage your endurance and energy for the long haul.

But that's not all. Here's the big secret: fresh eyes.

You must *create* distance, perspective and space for objectivity if you expect to generate quality – and sometimes in the face of business delivery pressures. Ask – are you delivering to a meagre budget or a good standard? If it's the former, survival requires you to have plenty of template solutions to hand (though repurposing templates isn't particularly creative). If it's the latter, plan and negotiate the right budget.

Fresh eyes reveal glaring shortcomings and flaws which just weren't visible with your head in the weeds. Take it from the world's greatest creators – never mistake a first draft or beta for 'good.' A starter? Perhaps.

Distance from your work fires up the executive centre in the brain (the part that does the thinking), versus the amygdala (the fearing part which paralyses creatives).

You may recall that we said simplicity and essence were vital in communicating ideas powerfully: **well, remember that time is the great distiller of ideas.** When you sleep on something, for instance, the brain prunes away the noise from the day and structures your memories, leaving just the necessary and viable neurone connections in place. Have you ever noticed that when you come back to something the following day, or after a week (or any period) you can instantly see ways to improve it? That's because your brain literally clears fog when you give it the time to do so. Use that clearing and ask: what features of your creation stand the test of time?

Just *don't* use this stage as an excuse to procrastinate. Get on with stage 6 and loop back round if you need to.

The big challenge at work is that most corporates aren't set up to be particularly creative (though they may tout it as part of their DNA). By and large they live on efficient dependable performance through prescribed processes, delivered right first time and to fixed timescales. All of this points to template filling and, at best, creativity with a small c. Process pays bills whereas creativity is inherently risky, and its outcomes often the result of happy accidents.

My advice is to pick an aspect of your work which is less time bound and perhaps off a budget radar, in order to hone your creative skills. There's a good chance no one else will see opportunity the way you do, so you may be left alone to do what you want with it. It's essential to create space around you if you want to be more creative.

6. **Package, iterate and evolve your way to the best answer**

This is especially important if you want an eventual leap of faith from your intended audience. The point can be illustrated by a tech example I've used before – Apple got its customers used to Siri as a fun add-on to the iPhone before they launched the first Apple watch, based entirely on voice-interaction. This meant the audience had adjusted ahead of time. So, it's essential to package ideas that others can consume without effort on their part.

Okay, so before we leave creativity, you might have notices some of its inherent paradoxes:

- You often have to create *several* options to a solution, before finding the *one* which works. Are these several *failures* on the road to *success*? To *succeed* you have to allow for some *failure*. Just make sure you fail safely, so you have the courage to go on
- Creatives must *respect* convention, yet *innovate* convention
- You have to *deliver* solutions, yet give them time to *emerge*

- Equally, it's good to keep the *time pressure* on, yet *loosen control*
- Finally, solution teams require *diversity*, yet must be *aligned*

There are, no doubt, more to add to the list. Now, go create!

Questions

1. What creative process (or hope for the best) do you apply in your work? ....

2. Which elements of the creative process above could you apply more consistently? ....

Strategy #38: Cultivate Options and Commitment for Resilience

Truly impactful people bake resilience into the way they operate. **They create options for what they don't control and commit deeply to what they do control.**

When we're not calling the shots, fixation to our own expectations drives a wedge into our charisma. But options negate that attachment and permit indifference to the myriad things to which we have no rights.

When 1 out of 10 options in our portfolio goes bad, the ship doesn't sink, and we're not blown off course.

We're trying to avoid a single failure point, mimicking nature, with its infinite options for sustainability. That makes it indifferent and infinitely resilient to any single outcome (us, in effect). Putting all your eggs into one basket, however, or betting the farm is the total opposite in this situation – great for a story, though bad news for your sustainability.

I'm not suggesting you work on infinite options – that would simply be a lack of focus.

What is unbeatable, however, are 2-3 equally good options which create redundancy in decisions and choice. The options should ideally be mutually exclusive to be truly robust in high-stakes major events or expectations. That could be job options, income sources, financing options and even supporters for your pitch or agenda. Rather than attaching yourself to a singular failure point or outcome, cultivate options to see the world with objectivity, maturity and perspective.

When it comes to option building, then, you have to learn, to some extent, to throw things at the wall and see what sticks. That probably describes the fortunes of two of the most successful tech products in recent years – SMS messages and App stores. Neither started with these products touting the success they would eventually become.

So, for resilience, then, read options when you're not in charge. Be creative and engage diversity.

An example of how you might do that (with a résumé) is shown below.

A Résumé – Re-Packaging and Combining Diverse Expertise Creates Options

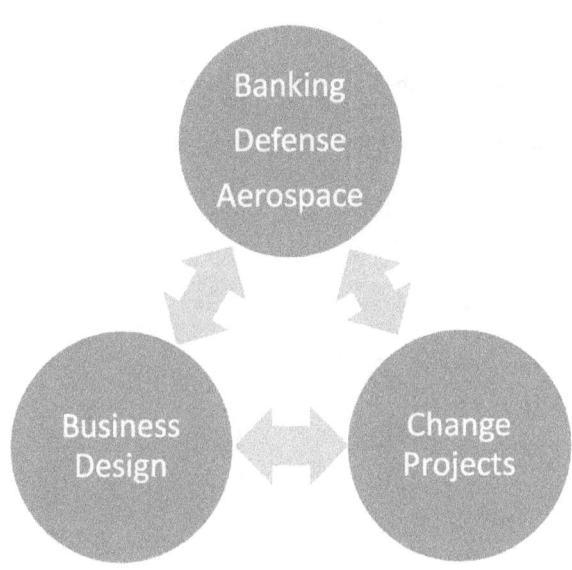

But the same indifference can be fatal when you do have control.

That, instead is where you need commitment – the sort which scares rivals away; the sort which propels you around the competence cycle; the sort, in which others see trust, dependability and resolution; the sort where you take full responsibility for your outcomes.

Questions

1. How can you create diverse expertise in your résumé or work and combine them to create new options? ....

2. Do you cultivate commitment in your work? ....

Strategy #39: Learn How to Learn

So, you now want to move up the competence curve we discussed earlier and get creative.

You'd better learn how to learn.

When you're opening up to the world again, during the diversity stage, you're giving yourself the opportunity to observe and to learn. It's your chance to *create* the capabilities you'll need to get to the next level.

This learning requires:

- Active engagement (read: attention). When you're learning effectively, you should be suffering at least a little mental discomfort, knowing that learning is work for the brain. Conversely, a state of comfort suggests you may not be doing anything new to you. Some learning experts even suggest you're best served throwing yourself into the deep end, into what's known as *the learning pit*, where you're temporarily disorientated by what you come across and have to figure out which way's back up the learning curve. This state of affairs gets your full attention which is why it's useful to learning. It's also why enduring Stage 2 of the competence cycle is essential for learning deeply, however uncomfortable it feels at the time.

- Periodic forced recall – or repetition (at intervals of 1 week, then 2 weeks, then 1 month, for instance)
- Forced connections in your head, explaining what you've learnt in your own words
- Testing your understanding with problem solving.

This quadruples your recall compared to straight cramming and is the number one advice from learning experts. Your aim is to test outputs, not to simply recognize inputs on a page.

What you need to remember is that learning is *a physical process* inside the brain.

A substance called myelin wraps itself around new nerve connections and cements new thought pathways that are formed when you *do* something new. New myelin is added over the connection when it's repeatedly used – so frequent *doing* is key. *Neurons that fire together, wire together,* goes the old saying in neuroscience, and is another way of saying that *practice make perfect*. Practice, in turn, is the essence of habit which we talked about earlier, reinforcing further still, the concept that you get more of whatever you focus on.

This physical process of learning is only activated when *doing*. It doesn't happen when listening, reading, watching, or anything passive.

Passive activity, like reading, is called memorizing, and that's not the same thing as learning.

Start by being *fully* attentive to what you are doing.

Multi-tasking is shown to diminish recall, so you don't stand a chance at learning that way.

Learning or memorizing with music or noise in the background may well be like driving with the brakes on. It can, however, be useful to distract you from grumbling when doing necessary but mind-numbing crud.

Now, the actual moment of learning is quite specific. It's when you're correcting errors or mistakes.

Correcting mistakes creates moments of learning. Not spotting *and* not correcting mistakes means you're standing still or not extending yourself sufficiently.

I hope this realization is a big release for self-effacing perfectionists out there. Making and correcting errors is quite simply learning and not anything substandard, so don't be hard on yourself when you feel incompetent.

Equally, though, passing off mistakes for learning is never a good idea.

Remember we said that sleep induces synaptic pruning – that is, the brain clears noise and debris from the day, structuring our memories for optimum recall? It goes without saying then, that sufficient sleep underpins effective learning.

It's helpful to learn only what you need to know in order to perform a current activity or whatever's next on your plate. That'll keep you focused on doing what you can (while allowing ideas to percolate in the subconscious like a tea bag in water), rather than absorbing useless information that you can't use – until you've forgotten it!

But new research from Radboud University Medical Centre in The Netherlands goes further, showing that exercise around four hours after learning, can also improve memory consolidation and retention.

Finally, we return to technology and its place in learning. A study from Dartmouth College in the UK suggests that reading from screens leads us to search and focus on easily digestible facts, rather than meanings. It appears that the brain doesn't process high level abstract ideas when reading on screens, perhaps because we've trained ourselves to use quick glances for information online. Consider, then, using hard copy to support your learning.

Questions

1. Which parts of the learning process do you avoid? ....

2. How can you ensure you'll do it more often? ....

3. Would you benefit from learning before doing to give ideas time to percolate? ....

Summary E

Okay, so that completes the final part of our productivity circle – diversity.

We leant why creatives own the future and how we need distraction and a range of experience to find our creative input. We then looked at creativity and the creative process. We went on to cultivate options amongst diversity, then read how to learn effectively.

All of that is aimed at helping you get more creative in doing whatever you do.

If you embrace diversity well, you'll be infinitely more creative and resilient in the face of challenges.

Closing Remarks

I hope the strategies in this book have given you the tools to do the right things and to do those things right – for big impact.

We've learnt powerful strategies to:

- **Choose what to focus on and prevent the choice of others from dominating**: #18: Set Good Goals, A, #19: Triage, #20: 1-3 Ways to Spend your Time
- **Do what you do really well**: #25: Avoid Willpower: Consistency is King, C. Batching, D. Focus and Do the Work, #31: Beware the Multi-tasking Myth
- **Limit or avoid frivolous distractions**: #21: The 80:20 Pareto Principle, #26: Limit your Choice, #28: Don't Manage Email, #29: Focus with Pomodoro and Internet Blockers
- **Use tailored systems, processes, habits and routines to achieve what you want**: B. Habits & Routine, #23: Trust the Process, #24: Make Winning Decisions and Choices, #38: Cultivate Options
- **Push through obstacles in your path**: #27: Be Grateful on Cue, #30: Remain Present, #32: Rise Early, #33: Manage your Energy, #34: Speed Date, #35: Persist with Competence, #36: Rest and Play before Work
- **Create without relying on blind faith, hope, motivation or vision:** E. Diversity, #37: Get Creative
- **Thrive and take it to the next level**: #22: Know your Key Success Factors, #39: Learning.

Okay, now just go and practice these things! Only deliberate practice – and correcting your mistakes – makes perfect.

I hope you've learnt that simply showing up at work and quietly doing the external stuff in your job to the best of your ability is the least of your challenges for creating big impact. Those climbing the ladder will be throwing all of the above – and more – at you, whether or not you are aware of it.

Remember also that learning is doing, not just reading or memorizing. Take one strategy at a time and make it part of your habit or routine. Incorporate another when the previous one's under your belt. Finally, dip back in and find something new on another commute as you progress.

I'm confident that the material will be life changing if you systematically incorporate it into your life, because I've seen that in everyone I've coached.

This series is certain to benefit others, so don't hold back – share the strategies, whether in the office or at home, and help others get on track.

Talk to your boss, mentors, coaches, colleagues, family, or friends, and ask them to help you build an objective picture of *you* – from their perspective.

Please also be sure to review the book – describing how it helped you – on Amazon, iBooks, Kobo, or wherever you purchased it. That helps others to discover it and also provides feedback for future improvements.

Finally, if you want to join a training program based on the content of this book, or if you require coaching, or even if you just want more impact strategies, look for other books in the series at 60strategies.com or follow the links in the front of this book.

Good luck, and let me know how you are doing via the series' website, at 60strategies.com.

If you haven't already, go back and discover how to be Self-aware and manage Behavior & Motivation in Volume 1

You're now ready to discover how to Communicate & Lead with Power & Presence with Volume 3

Get the books @ 60strategies.com

www.ingramcontent.com/pod-product-compliance
Lightning Source LLC
Chambersburg PA
CBHW071428180526
45170CB00001B/263